FLYING
HIGH

Philadelphia Eagles
World Champions

NICKY BRILLOWSKI, *Book Design*
KITTY GRIGSBY, *Cover Design*

ISBN: 978-1-940056-60-9

Printed in the United States of America
KCI Sports Publishing   3340 Whiting Avenue, Suite 5   Stevens Point, WI 54481
Phone: 1-800-697-3756   Fax: 715-344-2668
www.kcisports.com

CONTENTS

UNFORGETTABLE

Philadelphia Eagles – World Champions!
Sounds pretty good doesn't it? Philly fans have waited 58 long years to utter those words, and finally, the Eagles are back on top. Let the celebration begin!

It is an honor to write an introduction to such a historic season. This was a victory that had been months in the making. Following the Eagles 7-9 season in 2016, GM Howie Roseman headed into the offseason with one goal in mind—building a team that could win Super Bowl 52.

Mission accomplished.

On their way to Super Bowl 52 this Eagles team overcame a series of injuries that gutted the roster and landed numerous players on injured reserve including second-year quarterback Carson Wentz who through 12 weeks was putting up MVP-like numbers.

The perseverance, teamwork and will to win that made up the DNA of this Eagles team was on full display week after week, resulting in a season of highlights, including Jake Elliott's 61-yard field goal as time expired to beat the NY Giants in the season opener. Or the impressive road win against Carolina that made the league sit up and take notice. Or the dominant performance put forth in Dallas as they rolled over the Cowboys on Sunday Night Football. And who will ever forget the NFC Championship win over the favored Minnesota Vikings? The official game attendance was 69,596, but that number may well grow over the years as Philadelphia fans happily reminisce about that "I was there" game for years to come.

In the following pages *Flying High* proudly brings you on a trip down memory lane of this championship season that came to its jubilant conclusion with the Super Bowl victory over a very talented New England Patriots team.

Our heartfelt congratulations go out to Eagles owner Jeff Lurie, GM Howie Roseman, Coach Doug Pederson and his staff, and the entire team on their incredible accomplishments this season. Celebrate this season Eagles fans, and save this book to revisit the Eagles' magical moments and unforgettable team – both stars and role players – who rewarded your faith with a NFL Championship.

Congratulations Eagles! Let's do it again soon. ∎

Eagles quarterback Carson Wentz (11) looks to pass.
AP Photo

EAGLES
REDSKINS

30
17

Sept. 10 vs. Washington   FedEx Field   Landover, Maryland

Eagles defensive tackle Fletcher Cox (91) returns a fourth quarter fumble for a touchdown. *AP Photo*

Eagles roll in Season Opener

Carson Wentz put on a magic act evading pressure, the Philadelphia Eagles' defense ratcheted up its pass rush and the result was the end of a losing streak against the Washington Redskins and a Gatorade bath for coach Doug Pederson.

Behind two touchdowns from Wentz and four sacks of Kirk Cousins, the Eagles beat the Redskins 30-17 in a sloppy, mistake-filled season opener between the NFC East rivals.

Wentz threw for 307 yards and also had an interception returned for a touchdown but made fewer errors than Cousins, who was picked off at the goal line and fumbled twice.

Eagles receiver Nelson Agholor (13) makes the reception on what would end up being a 58-yard touchdown play.
AP Photo

Wentz ducked and darted away from two sacks, scrambled away from a few more defenders, managed to find decent footing, and bombed a pass along the left side to Eagles wide receiver Nelson Agholor. His receiver would do the rest, shaking off Redskins safety D.J. Swearinger to cap off the 58-yard catch-and-run touchdown that gave the Eagles their first score of the season.

"A lot of it honestly is instinct. They ran a good coverage and just kind of things broke down and just made plays," Wentz said. "But that's something we've talked about all offseason. 'Hey guys, never die out there. Always stay alive. Get open.' And Nelson did a great job and I think we had another couple open guys as well and that's just a thing we'll kind of continually work on and be a big part of our game."

"I don't know how the guy does it," left tackle Jason Peters said of Wentz, who was 26 of 39. "He's just got a knack for feeling pressure coming and he rolls out of it, he gets out of it and makes a play down the field."

Although it was the much-improved Agholor who finished off the offense's play of the day, tight end Zach Ertz was Wentz's favorite target on the afternoon. Ertz hauled in eight catches to lead the team with 93 yards receiving including a tremendous 23-yard catch over the middle on third-and-10 after another remarkable Wentz scramble.

Wentz already looks significantly more comfortable in his sophomore season leading the franchise. He made several deep tries down the field, far different from than the multiple short checkdown passes Wentz threw all last season.

"I think it just shows that we're aggressive. Coach (Doug Pederson) is going to be

Eagles defensive tackle Timmy Jernigan (93) and defensive end Brandon Graham (55) sack Washington Redskins quarterback Kirk Cousins (8). *AP Photo*

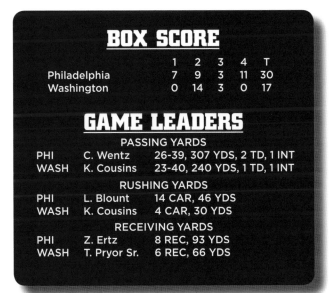

BOX SCORE

	1	2	3	4	T
Philadelphia	7	9	3	11	30
Washington	0	14	3	0	17

GAME LEADERS

PASSING YARDS
PHI	C. Wentz	26-39, 307 YDS, 2 TD, 1 INT
WASH	K. Cousins	23-40, 240 YDS, 1 TD, 1 INT

RUSHING YARDS
PHI	L. Blount	14 CAR, 46 YDS
WASH	K. Cousins	4 CAR, 30 YDS

RECEIVING YARDS
PHI	Z. Ertz	8 REC, 93 YDS
WASH	T. Pryor Sr.	6 REC, 66 YDS

aggressive. We're going to be aggressive. We're not going to just sit back and wait. We're going to try and make plays early and often and I love that about Coach Pederson. I love the way he called the game today. Came out aggressive right away and kind of just stayed on it," Wentz said.

Cousins finished 23 of 40 for 240 yards with an interception and two fumbles, the second of which was forced by Brandon Graham and returned 20 yards for a touchdown by Fletcher Cox in the final minutes, putting the game away.

Cousins had a TD pass to third-down back Chris Thompson, but much of the afternoon was done in by drops and other offensive blunders.

The Eagles snapped a five-game skid against the Redskins going back to Sept. 9, 2014, and won at FedEx Field for the first time since 2013.

"We've been talking all week about kind of getting the monkey off our back down here and really against the Redskins," Pederson said. "It was just the old setup on the sideline, and I got the bath. Appreciate it, but a little sticky. ■

Kansas City Chiefs tight end Travis Kelce (87) leaps over Eagles cornerback Rasul Douglas (32) after a reception in the second half.   *AP Photo*

CHIEFS
EAGLES

27
20

REGULAR
SEASON
GAME

Sept. 17 vs. Kansas City   Arrowhead Stadium   Kansas City, Missouri

Kansas City Chiefs defensive back Daniel Sorensen (49) leaps as he attempts to tackle Eagles quarterback Carson Wentz (11). *AP Photo*

Chiefs hold on to beat Eagles 27-20

The Kansas City Chiefs followed their offensive-minded upset of the New England Patriots by leaning on their stout, opportunistic defense to upend the Philadelphia Eagles.

Two wins. Two vastly different ways to achieve them.

"No two games area alike in this league," said Alex Smith, who threw for 251 yards and a touchdown in their 27-20 victory on Sunday. "You have to find ways to make adjustments."

WORLD CHAMPIONS

(13)

Eagles wide receiver Alshon Jeffery (17) fights for the ball with Chiefs defensive backs Daniel Sorensen (49), Kenneth Acker (25) and Eric Murray (21) on a Hail Mary pass thrown by Eagles quarterback Carson Wentz on the last play of the game. *AP Photo*

Six sacks and two interceptions is a good place to start.

The Chiefs (2-0) simply outscored the Patriots in their season opener last week, but they needed three sacks and a pick from defensive tackle Chris Jones , solid play in a secondary missing star safety Eric Berry, and some big plays down the stretch to keep the Eagles (1-1) at bay.

Travis Kelce had eight catches for 103 yards and a somersaulting go-ahead touchdown grab with 6:25 left in the game. Rookie Kareem Hunt followed his record-setting debut by running for 81 yards and two scores, the second of them giving Kansas City a 27-13 lead and seemingly putting the game away.

But Carson Wentz hit Nelson Agholor for an answering score with 14 seconds left, and Trey Burton jumped on the onside kick a few seconds later to give the Eagles one last throw

to the end zone.

The Chiefs' defense stood tall once more: Wentz unloaded from just inside the 50-yard line, but his pass bounced off the hands of a couple defenders and fell incomplete as time expired.

"The takeaway is you're right there, a team that lit the scoreboard up in Week 1 in New England,'" Eagles coach Doug Pederson said. "But we got to get the run game fixed. It's a team effort. However the game plays out, we try to find a way to win at the end and mistakes obviously cost us today."

Wentz finished with 333 yards and two touchdowns passing, despite facing relentless pressure all afternoon. The spunky quarterback also led the Eagles with 55 yards rushing.

"He's going to be one of the great ones in the league," Chiefs linebacker Justin

Eagles tight end Zach Ertz (86) runs away from Kansas City Chiefs defenders after catching a deflected pass. *AP Photo*

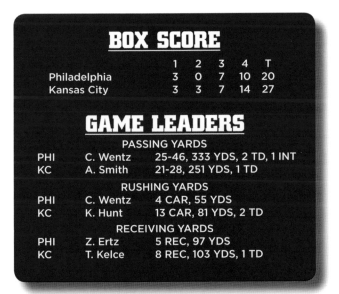

BOX SCORE

	1	2	3	4	T
Philadelphia	3	0	7	10	20
Kansas City	3	3	7	14	27

GAME LEADERS

PASSING YARDS

PHI	C. Wentz	25-46, 333 YDS, 2 TD, 1 INT
KC	A. Smith	21-28, 251 YDS, 1 TD

RUSHING YARDS

PHI	C. Wentz	4 CAR, 55 YDS
KC	K. Hunt	13 CAR, 81 YDS, 2 TD

RECEIVING YARDS

PHI	Z. Ertz	5 REC, 97 YDS
KC	T. Kelce	8 REC, 103 YDS, 1 TD

Houston said. "He's very mobile, very calm in the pocket. It's tough to rush a guy like that that's real mobile in the pocket. He can spin move and get out of trouble."

The Chiefs led 6-3 at halftime, and it was still 13-13 in the fourth quarter when Wentz threw a pass that bounced off Houston and into the arms of Chris Jones. The pick gave Kansas City the ball deep in Eagles territory, and Kelce hurdled into the end zone five plays later.

The Eagles got after it on defense, but didn't get off the field at critical times in the defeat.

"We did some good things," defensive end Brandon Graham said of a defense that sacked Kansas City quarterback Alex Smith four times and limited the Chiefs to 344 total net yards. "But it wasn't good enough. We had it right there and we couldn't put it away. ∎

A view of Lincoln Financial Field prior to the Eagles 2017 home opener versus the New York Giants. *AP Photo*

EAGLES
GIANTS

27
24

Sept. 24 vs. New York   Lincoln Financial Field   Philadelphia, Pennsylvania

Eagles kicker Jake Elliott (4) kicks the game-winning 61-yard field goal as time expires. *AP Photo*

Elliott's 61-yard field goal lifts

Eagles in home opener

Jake Elliott ran over to coaches and begged for a chance to try the longest field goal in team history.

They said yes - and he nailed it.

Elliott kicked a 61-yarder as the clock expired to lift the Philadelphia Eagles to a 27-24 victory over the New York Giants.

Carson Wentz tossed a 19-yard pass to Alshon Jefferyto to set up Elliott's kick, the longest game-winner in NFL history for a

WORLD CHAMPIONS

Eagles rookie running back Corey Clement (30) dives into the end zone for his first career touchdown. *AP Photo*

rookie and a franchise record. Elliott was a fifth-round pick by the Bengals and joined the Eagles after Caleb Sturgis was injured in Week 1. He was carried off the field by two teammates.

"I'm thankful I had the opportunity to try it," Elliott said. "I wanted it."

Elliott missed from 52 yards earlier in the game and last week missed from 30 yards and shanked an extra point.

"It's surreal, but it's the life of a kicker," Elliott said. "You have ups and downs and you move onto next week."

Eagles coach Doug Pederson conferred with special teams coach Dave Fipp before sending Elliott on the field.

"I had so much confidence in him," Pederson said.

Eli Manning threw three touchdown passes in the fourth quarter, including a 77-yard score to Sterling Shepard, but Philadelphia (2-1) rallied twice.

Elliott hit a 46-yard field goal to tie it with 51 seconds left after Aldrick Rosas kicked a 41-yarder to put the Giants ahead.

The Giants (0-3) hadn't scored 20 points in eight straight games before Manning led them to 21 in a span of 5:21. He tossed TD passes of 10 yards and 4 yards to Odell Beckham Jr. to tie it at 14. Manning then connected over the middle to Shepard, who broke a couple tackles and sprinted all the way for a 21-14 lead.

But Philadelphia answered quickly.

A 36-yard penalty for pass interference on Eli Apple put the ball at the 15 and rookie Corey Clement ran in on the next play for his first career TD to make it 21-all.

The running game showed up for the Eagles at the right time.

Wendell Smallwood had 12 carries for 71 punishing yards and LeGarrette Blount picked up 67 yards and a touchdown on 12 carries. Rookie Corey Clement scored for the first time in his young career on a 15-yard run to tie the

New York Giants cornerback Janoris Jenkins (20) defends a pass intended for Eagles wide receiver Alshon Jeffery (17). *AP Photo*

BOX SCORE

	1	2	3	4	T
New York	0	0	0	24	24
Philadelphia	0	7	7	13	27

GAME LEADERS

PASSING YARDS
NYG	E. Manning	35-47, 366 YDS, 3 TD, 2 INT
PHI	C. Wentz	21-31, 176 YDS, 1 TD

RUSHING YARDS
NYG	O. Darkwa	7 CAR, 22 YDS
PHI	W. Smallwood	12 CAR, 71 YDS

RECEIVING YARDS
NYG	S. Shepard	7 REC, 133 YDS, 1 TD
PHI	A. Jeffery	4 REC, 56 YDS

game 21-21 in the fourth quarter.

"We got into a little bit of a rhythm. The guys up front did a terrific job and I just followed them," Smallwood said. "It was fun getting the carries and staying with it."

Head coach Doug Pederson announced that running back Darren Sproles will miss the remainder of the 2017 season after suffering a torn ACL and a broken forearm on the same play during the win against the Giants.

"It's a devastating loss obviously with the punt return, the special teams aspect of it," Pederson said. "So we'll look at everything the next day or so. It's going to have to be the next man up mentality."▪

WIDE RECEIVER
ALSHON JEFFERY

A Quiet Confidence

Alshon Jeffery speaks softly during interviews, with his head down, shuffling his feet and smiling every now and then.

And yet, if you strain close enough to hear him, you can sense why the Eagles' wide receiver is so admired by his teammates, and why he has become a leader on the team.

Jeffery exudes a quiet confidence, which he isn't afraid to express. It just doesn't come across as braggadocio, like it did with former Eagles wide receiver Freddie Mitchell, who famously called his hands "great" after a 2005 playoff game against Minnesota.

Jeffery has praised his catching ability on a few occasions already this season, most recently when asked about his 3-yard touchdown catch on Sunday against the Giants in the Eagles' 34-29 win.

"I just think I did a great job with getting open," Jeffery said. "Nick [Foles] made a great throw. I made a great catch. It's a read route. It was just watching how the defense covers. I was the last option. It was a great play."

Against the Giants, Foles threw a pass into the end zone to Nelson Agholor, who climbed over the back of the Giants defender and took the ball away from him.

Jeffery came over to celebrate. He pretended to be a basketball player throwing an alley-oop pass that Agholor pretended to slam through the basket.

"He dunked on his [butt]," Jeffery said about Agholor's catch. "That's why I threw it up to him. It was like Blake Griffin. CP3 to Blake Griffin."

Jeffery was referring to the former Los Angeles Clippers teammates in point guard Chris Paul and forward Blake Griffin, who were known for their alley-oop dunks.

Alshon Jeffery led the Eagles with nine touchdown receptions during the regular season. *AP Photo*

Jeffery warms up prior to a game against the Los Angeles Rams. *AP Photo*

What does this all have to do with football?

For one, Jeffery said this is the most fun he has ever had in his six seasons in the NFL, the first five with the Chicago Bears. "We're winning man," he said. "That's all that matters."

Secondly, it shows that the wide receiver unit is a tight-knit one, and the receivers don't mind sacrificing their stats.

A lot of that comes from Jeffery, but not necessarily through words.

"I'd say he's quiet, but he's not," fellow receiver Torrey Smith said. "He's more laid back than quiet. He'll get on guys, absolutely. Everyone has their own way of leading."

Jeffery has certainly sacrificed. He has 56 catches for 781 yards as the Eagles prepare for their game Monday night against the Oakland Raiders. He'll finish well short of his career highs in catches (89) and yards (1,421), both set in 2013. Jeffery is one touchdown catch away from tying his career high of 10 set in 2014.

This came after Jeffery signed a one-year contract with the Eagles last spring as a free agent. In essence, Jeffery was betting on himself to have a good season in order to get a lucrative long-term contract.

But Jeffery won't come close to 100 catches, and will most likely fall short of 1,000 yards, which typically are benchmarks for top NFL receivers. It didn't matter. The Eagles signed Jeffery to a four-year deal worth as much as $52 million earlier this month.

And it wasn't because of Jeffery's touchdown dance choreography.

"I think it stands out in the way he practices and the way he plays," Eagles coach Doug Pederson said. "Maybe he's not the most vocal guy, but he definitely leads by example." ∎

Eagles tackle Lane Johnson (65) celebrates in the end zone after a touchdown. *AP Photo*

EAGLES
CHARGERS

26
24

REGULAR
SEASON
GAME

Oct. 1 vs. Los Angeles   StubHub Center   Carson, California

Eagles running back LaGarrette Blount (29) uses a stiff arm to break away from the Chargers Desmond King (20) during a second half run. *AP Photo*

Blount powers Eagles past

winless Chargers

LeGarrette Blount burst through the line, escaped an ankle tackle and powered into the secondary, where he stiff-armed a Chargers rookie twice to cap a rampaging 68-yard run.

"From my vantage point, it was one of the most impressive runs I've seen in my life," Philadelphia quarterback Carson Wentz said.

The Eagles are off to a fast start after another smash-mouth victory in a road stadium that felt like home.

Wentz passed for 242 yards, Blount rushed

WORLD CHAMPIONS

(25)

Eagles receiver Alshon Jeffery (17) scores on a 8-yard touchdown reception.
AP Photo

for 136 and the Eagles jumped to a big early lead before hanging on for a 26-24 victory over the winless Los Angeles Chargers.

Blount's 68-yard run eventually led to Wendell Smallwood's TD dive with 9:14 to play after a penalty on Los Angeles' Darius Philon kept the Eagles alive.

"I know what I can do," Blount said. "I know I'm one of the better backs in this league. I'm always going to run with that passion and that confidence."

"They wore down in the fourth quarter," Eagles left tackle Jason Peters said of the Chargers. "Matter of fact, they wore down in the third quarter going into the fourth, and we took advantage of it."

Rookie Jake Elliott kicked four field goals for the Eagles, who had thousands of vocal fans in the Chargers' temporary arena while they won on the road for the second time in 10 tries. Those fans roared their approval particularly after Philadelphia ran out the game with a bruising 13-play drive over the final 6:44, simply refusing to give a final chance to the Chargers' offense.

"Even though we're four games in, this team is really beginning to believe in themselves, believe in each other," head coach Doug Pederson said.

Playing without Fletcher Cox and several injured defensive regulars, the Eagles matched last season's 3-1 start. The running game was impressive: Blount combined with Smallwood and Corey Clement to rush for 200 yards, with Blount picking up 88 yards in the fourth quarter, along with the clinching first down on that clock-chewing drive.

"It's two weeks in a row now that he's done

Los Angeles Chargers wide receiver Tyrell Williams (16) is upended by Eagles linebacker Mychal Kendricks (95). *AP Photo*

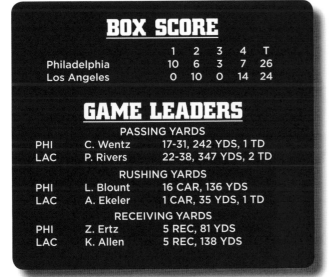

BOX SCORE

	1	2	3	4	T
Philadelphia	10	6	3	7	26
Los Angeles	0	10	0	14	24

GAME LEADERS

PASSING YARDS

PHI	C. Wentz	17-31, 242 YDS, 1 TD
LAC	P. Rivers	22-38, 347 YDS, 2 TD

RUSHING YARDS

PHI	L. Blount	16 CAR, 136 YDS
LAC	A. Ekeler	1 CAR, 35 YDS, 1 TD

RECEIVING YARDS

PHI	Z. Ertz	5 REC, 81 YDS
LAC	K. Allen	5 REC, 138 YDS

a great job," Pederson said. "Big guy at the end of the game, you saw the big long run. I don't think he has anything to prove, it's the guy that I knew that we were getting back in the spring."

"I had a pretty good day," Blount said after his biggest day yet for his new team. "Running behind the O-line I run behind, it's pretty hard not to have a good day."

Rookie Austin Ekeler rushed for a 35-yard score on his first NFL carry and Hunter Henry made a one-handed TD catch during the Chargers' fourth-quarter surge.

Philadelphia ran out the clock after Henry's TD catch, making a time-consuming drive that ended in the Victory formation.

"We're running the ball, we're being physical, and it's wearing defenses down," center Jason Kelce said. "What we did there is exactly what you hope to do – run out the clock, keep the chains moving, and end it by kneeling down." ▪

Eagles wide receiver Nelson Agholor (13) celebrates a touchdown with running back LeGarrette Blount (29) as quarterback Caron Wentz (11) joins the celebration. *AP Photo*

EAGLES 34
CARDINALS 7

Oct. 8 vs. Arizona   Lincoln Financial Field   Philadelphia, Pennsylvania

Quarterback Carson Wentz delivers one of his three first quarter touchdown passes. *AP Photo*

Eagles Win Third Straight

Carson Wentz calls third downs the "money down." Cha-ching.

Wentz threw a career-best four touchdown passes and the Philadelphia Eagles continued their impressive start with a 34-7 victory over the Arizona Cardinals.

Wentz tossed three scoring passes on three consecutive attempts in the first quarter, including 59 yards to Torrey Smith, 11 yards to Zach Ertz and 15 yards to Trey Burton. He connected with Nelson Agholor for a 72-yard TD in the third quarter that left six-time Pro Bowl cornerback Patrick Peterson shouting on the sideline.

WORLD CHAMPIONS

Eagles wide receiver Torrey Smith (82) celebrates in the end zone after a touchdown with Alshon Jeffery (17), quarterback Carson Went (11), tight end Zach Ertz (86) and running back LeGarrette Blount (29). *AP Photo*

The Eagles (4-1) have won three straight games.

Wentz was 11 for 12 for 225 yards and three TDs on third down.

"To be that efficient, that's huge," Wentz said.

Carson Palmer and Arizona's one-dimensional offense were held to 279 yards. The Cardinals (2-3) have alternated losses and wins since Week 1.

Wentz torched a secondary that features Peterson and Tyrann Mathieu, finishing 21 of 30 for 304 yards. Peterson held Alshon Jeffery to three catches for 31 yards, but

Wentz spread the ball around.

The Eagles entered with the NFL's second-best third-down offense and converted their first four chances, including two of Wentz's early TDs.

"We got ourselves into some winnable downs and we weren't able to get off the field," Peterson said.

On the opening drive, Wentz tossed a 12 yard pass to Ertz on third-and-11 and a 16-yard pass to Jeffery on another third-and-11. Then he found Burton on a fade for a 7-0 lead.

Wentz's TD pass to Ertz came on third-and-6 to make it 14-0. He hit Smith in stride

Eagles tight end Trey Burton (88) hauls in a 15-yard touchdown pass. *AP Photo*

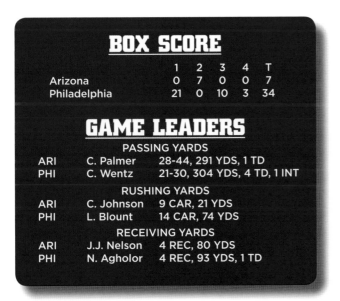

BOX SCORE

	1	2	3	4	T
Arizona	0	7	0	0	7
Philadelphia	21	0	10	3	34

GAME LEADERS

PASSING YARDS
ARI	C. Palmer	28-44, 291 YDS, 1 TD
PHI	C. Wentz	21-30, 304 YDS, 4 TD, 1 INT

RUSHING YARDS
ARI	C. Johnson	9 CAR, 21 YDS
PHI	L. Blount	14 CAR, 74 YDS

RECEIVING YARDS
ARI	J.J. Nelson	4 REC, 80 YDS
PHI	N. Agholor	4 REC, 93 YDS, 1 TD

on third-and-5 for a 21-0 lead.

"Our execution was pretty good, Carson made accurate throws and the guys did a nice job route running," coach Doug Pederson said.

The Cardinals finally got going when Palmer threw a 13-yard TD pass to John Brown to cut it to 21-7.

Agholor's TD catch was on third-and-19. He blew past safety Budda Baker, caught Wentz's perfect pass over the shoulder and used a spin move and stiff arm to reach the end zone.

"I shouldn't have been able to make the throw, but Jason Kelce made a great block on two guys," Wentz said about his center. "And then Nelly made the guy look silly."

Kenjon Barner had a 76-yard punt return to set up Philadelphia's second TD. Barner was signed after veteran Darren Sproles tore his ACL in Week 3. ∎

Eagles tight end Zak Ertz (86) snares a 17-yard touchdown pass as Panthers strong safety Mike Adams (29) defends. *AP Photo*

EAGLES 28
PANTHERS 23

Oct. 12 vs. Carolina   Bank of America Stadium   Charlotte, North Carolina

Carolina quarterback Cam Newton (1) gets pulled down by the Eagles Chris Long (56) and Malcolm Jenkins (27) during second half action. *AP Photo*

Statement made:

Eagles are for real

Carson Wentz said he saw some things from the Carolina Panthers he hadn't seen on film leading to three first-half sacks and plenty of pressure.

It didn't bother the Philadelphia Eagles' second-year quarterback.

Wentz came up big in a huge game, throwing for 222 yards and three touchdowns against one of the NFL's top defenses, and the Eagles beat the Panthers 28-23 on Thursday night to improve to an NFC-best 5-1.

"We kept backs in to handle their linebackers and we did

WORLD CHAMPIONS

33

Eagles safety Malcolm Jenkins (27) attempts to strip the ball away from Panthers running back Christian McCaffrey (22). *AP Photo*

a better job cleaning it up in the second half," said Wentz, who wasn't sacked in the second half.

The Eagles turned two interceptions deep in Carolina territory into 15 points. Wentz teamed with Zach Ertz on two touchdown passes, and LaGarrette Blount scored on a 2-point conversion run for an 18-10 lead in the third quarter. Wentz added a 24-yard scoring pass to Nelson Agholor in the fourth quarter.

"He's a great leader of this football team, even in his second year," Eagles coach Doug Pederson said about Wentz. "Guys really respect the way he plays. It's exciting to see that."

Another win on the road is huge for Wentz and the Eagles, especially when comparing where they are now to where they were at this time last year. Wentz believes they are a different team all around and that is what is bringing them such success.

"Having a year together with this team, under (Coach Doug Pederson), myself, and everything, we're just built differently. We have different character makeup in that locker room," Wentz said. "We just have a bunch of guys that believe that no matter the situation we can find a way to win a ballgame."

Cam Newton threw three interceptions for Carolina (4-2).

The first two interceptions came inside Carolina's 20, but weren't Newton's fault. He was hit by Fletcher Cox as he released one pass, and running back Jonathan Stewart bobbled another pass resulting in a pick. Newton's third interception - by Jalen

Mills with 3:06 left - ended a chance for the go-ahead score.

Carolina had one last shot to win, but turned it over on downs at midfield.

"We gave them layups, giving them the ball inside our 20," Newton said. "Against a good team like that, well that's not good ingredients to win. We can't put our defense in that type of position."

"We were up for the challenge. We prepared well on a short week and we played lights out today," said Eagles safety Rodney McLeod. "I'm really proud of everyone. To come in here and do it against this kind of team, man, that says a lot about our team."

Eagles wide receiver Alshon Jeffery (17) makes the catch after beating Panthers cornerback Kevin Seymour (27).
AP Photo

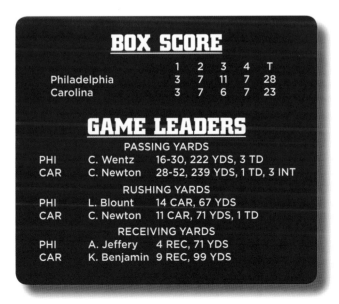

BOX SCORE

	1	2	3	4	T
Philadelphia	3	7	11	7	28
Carolina	3	7	6	7	23

GAME LEADERS

PASSING YARDS
PHI	C. Wentz	16-30, 222 YDS, 3 TD
CAR	C. Newton	28-52, 239 YDS, 1 TD, 3 INT

RUSHING YARDS
PHI	L. Blount	14 CAR, 67 YDS
CAR	C. Newton	11 CAR, 71 YDS, 1 TD

RECEIVING YARDS
PHI	A. Jeffery	4 REC, 71 YDS
CAR	K. Benjamin	9 REC, 99 YDS

Newton gave the Panthers a 10-3 lead on his 51st career touchdown rushing in the second quarter. He kept the ball on a read option and juked cornerback Rasul Douglas on the 16-yard run.

Douglas got revenge on Carolina's next possession, intercepting Newton's pass after Cox crashed into Newton as he was throwing, causing the ball to float high into the air.

After a two-game absence due to a calf injury, Cox returned and was a dominant force. Along with the tipped pass on Newton's interception, he also had a sack and two quarterback hurries. "There's no way I could sit him tonight," Pederson said. "It was too important to him." ▪

SAFETY
MALCOLM JENKINS

A Born Leader

It would have been easy for Malcolm Jenkins to get distracted this season.

After all, he's the perceived leader of the Eagles, a veteran who will express the players' concerns to coaches while also inspiring them with his words in the team huddle just after warm-ups.

He has also taken on a much bigger role this season in protesting racial injustices during the national anthem. There is also his work in the community and the clothing store he opened this year in Philadelphia.

And, oh yeah, his wife, Morrissa, had a baby daughter last week.

Through it all, Jenkins has had perhaps his most rewarding season both on the field and off.

"This has probably been my easiest season to lead since I've been in an Eagles uniform [beginning in 2014]," Jenkins said. "There have been other seasons where I felt like I had to stand up in front of the team almost every week. But this year, we've got so many veteran guys and so many unselfish guys that it's been easy. All I've had to do is really go be myself."

For Jenkins, that means giving his teammates just the right perspective on pretty much everything. Typically, that begins in the team huddle on the field just after warm-ups are completed.

It also happens in the locker rooms after games.

Eagles head coach Doug Pederson called on Jenkins to speak to the team after a game early in the season. After that, Pederson didn't have to ask.

"I think now the guys embrace it," Pederson said. "I think it's just him being Malcolm and being a leader of this football team, and being one of the guys that they look to for that leadership. He's embraced it and guys look forward to it, obviously. He's been good. He's got a lot of profound messages as you've seen. He speaks from the heart and he speaks truth."

That was evident when quarterback Carson

Eagles strong safety Malcolm Jenkins. *AP Photo*

Jenkins fires up teammates before a game with Washington. *AP Photo*

Wentz suffered a season-ending torn ACL against the Rams on Dec. 10. After the game, a 43-35 Eagles' win that clinched the NFC East, Jenkins spoke to the team. In a video posted by the team, with several expletives deleted, Jenkins essentially told his teammates that nothing changes, that the Super Bowl is still the expectation.

He ended it with the mantra the team has used this season: "We all we got, we all we need."

"That was great to hear a guy like Malcolm step up and give a speech like that," defensive tackle Fletcher Cox said. "When Malcolm's talking, every guy in that locker room is listening because he means it from his heart. His main message was, 'Let's stick together and we can do this.'"

So far, they have. Jenkins' play, despite everything going on around him, is among the biggest reasons why.

Jenkins was selected to his second Pro Bowl. And he is a key component on a defense that hasn't allowed a single point in the second half of both of the Eagles' playoff games.

It was a far cry from a three-game stretch in December, when the Eagles struggled defensively in a 24-10 loss to the Seattle Seahawks and in wins over the Rams and New York Giants (34-29).

Jenkins said that the defense wasn't worried then about falling apart.

"No, it was just Todd Gurley and Russell Wilson," Jenkins said with a laugh about the Rams running back and Seahawks quarterback, respectively.

And now?

"I feel like we're playing some of the best ball that we've played," Jenkins said. "As the season has gone on, we've figured out what we do best, what individual guys do best, and how to manipulate the defense to put us in good spots. And we've had to learn those lessons as the season has gone on ... So now, we feel like we're experts at our jobs individually and collectively." ∎

Eagles receiver Mack Hollins (10) looks in a 64-yard touchdown reception. *AP Photo*

EAGLES
REDSKINS

34
24

Oct. 23 vs. Washington   Lincoln Financial Field   Philadelphia, Pennsylvania

Eagles quarterback Carson Wentz (11) tosses one of four touchdown passes against the Washington Redskins. *AP Photo*

Wentz Leads Eagles
past Redskins

Carson Wentz stood tall in a collapsing pocket and kept making plays with his arm or legs.

Wentz tossed four touchdown passes, and the Philadelphia Eagles overcame losing nine-time Pro Bowl left tackle Jason Peters in a 34-24 win over the Washington Redskins on Monday night.

"You step up and go into make-a-play mode," Wentz said after making one highlight play after another in front of a national audience while cementing his status as a first-half MVP candidate.

The second-year quarterback threw for 268 yards and ran for a career-best 63 after a shaky start to lead the NFL-best Eagles (6-1) to their fifth straight win. But the victory was costly because Peters was carted off the field with a knee injury in the third quarter.

WORLD CHAMPIONS

39

Kirk Cousins threw for 303 and three TDs for the Redskins (3-3).

"Carson made some unbelievable plays there in crunch-time situations," Redskins coach Jay Gruden said. "We lost and it wasn't good enough by anybody, offensively."

The Eagles went three-and-out three times in their first four drives and had only 57 total yards before Wentz hit Mack Hollins in stride with a perfect 64-yard TD pass to tie it at 10.

That got the offense rolling.

Wentz connected with tight end Zach Ertz for 46 yards on the next series and found him again for a 4-yard TD pass to make it 17-10.

"Amazing," Ertz said when asked to describe Wentz's play this season. "He's playing at an unreal level, MVP-type level. I know a lot of people are saying that, but he's doing amazing things for this football team, amazing things for this city, so we're really glad to have him."

After getting the second-half kickoff, the Eagles drove 86 yards for another touchdown. Peters was injured during the series, and fans chanted his name while teammates surrounded the cart.

Wentz finished the drive off with a play that Peters would appreciate.

While being hit by two defenders and falling forward, Wentz lofted a 9-yard TD pass to Corey Clement.

"One of the best plays I've seen in a long time and by two young guys," Eagles coach Doug Pederson said. "To hang in there and take shot after shot, it's amazing to me."

Wentz fired a 10-yard TD pass to Nelson Agholor to expand the lead to 31-17. Wentz kept that drive alive by escaping a sack and running 17 yards on third-and-8.

"That's what makes him so special," right

Eagles running back Wendell Smallwood (28) goes airborne while trying to avoid a tackle by Redskins cornerback Quinton Dunbar (47). *AP Photo*

Eagles outside linebacker Kamu Grugier-Hill (54) hits Redskins wide receiver Jamison Crowder (80) knocking the ball free. *AP Photo*

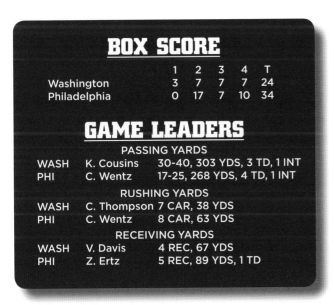

BOX SCORE

	1	2	3	4	T
Washington	3	7	7	7	24
Philadelphia	0	17	7	10	34

GAME LEADERS

PASSING YARDS
WASH	K. Cousins	30-40, 303 YDS, 3 TD, 1 INT
PHI	C. Wentz	17-25, 268 YDS, 4 TD, 1 INT

RUSHING YARDS
WASH	C. Thompson	7 CAR, 38 YDS
PHI	C. Wentz	8 CAR, 63 YDS

RECEIVING YARDS
WASH	V. Davis	4 REC, 67 YDS
PHI	Z. Ertz	5 REC, 89 YDS, 1 TD

tackle Lane Johnson said. "He has great field vision, and he's got something a lot of guys don't have."

Cousins tossed a 7-yard touchdown to Chris Thompson to give the Redskins a 10-3 lead. He connected with Jordan Reed on a 5-yard TD to cut the deficit to 24-17 and threw a 12-yard pass to Reed to cap the scoring.

The Eagles were penalized on four straight plays to start their first possession before Wentz was intercepted by Quinton Dunbar on a deep pass to Torrey Smith on second-and-31.

"It was the worst way to start a game that I've ever experienced," center Jason Kelce said. "It was just ... awful. I'm glad we got past it." ∎

Eagles defensive tackle Fletcher Cox reacts to his sack. *AP Photo*

EAGLES
49ERS

33
10

Oct. 29 vs. San Francisco   Lincoln Financial Field   Philadelphia, Pennsylvania

Eagles running back LaGarrette Blount (29) celebrates his fourth quarter touchdown. *AP Photo*

Eagles dominate 49ers

for sixth straight win

Even when they were sloppy, the Philadelphia Eagles won going away.

Carson Wentz tossed two touchdown passes, Jalen Mills had a pick-6 and the NFL-leading Eagles beat the winless San Francisco 49ers 33-10 on a rainy Sunday.

The Eagles (7-1) overcame a slow start on their way to a sixth straight win. The 49ers are 0-8 for the first time in franchise history.

"Offensively, we have to do better, but good teams find a way to win even when you play sluggish like we did," Wentz said. "Being 7-1, we like that. It's a good place to be. We just have to keep building,"

Eagles cornerback Jalen Mills (31) returns an interception 37-yards for a touchdown during second quarter action.
AP Photo

Wentz was 18 of 32 for 211 yards and one interception. He threw a 53-yard TD pass to Alshon Jeffery and 1-yard TD pass to Zach Ertz. The second-year pro leads the NFL with 19 TD passes, most by an Eagles quarterback through eight games.

The Eagles punted on six of their first eight possessions before opening it up in the third quarter.

Wentz hit Jeffery with a perfect pass to extend the lead to 27-7. After Derek Barnett blocked Robbie Gould's field goal, the Eagles drove 62 yards and LeGarrette Blount ran in from the 12 for a 33-7 lead.

"It's not the way the offense wanted to play," Eagles right tackle Lane Johnson said. "We came out slow and didn't execute. I'm just glad we battled because every game is not going to be perfect or look good. But we found a way to win and that's what teams do."

The 49ers stayed close until Wentz's

TD pass to Ertz was followed by Mills' interception. Mills picked 49ers quarterback C.J. Beathard's pass at the 37 and ran it back, zig-zagging his way to the end zone. Wentz connected with Jeffery on a 2-point conversion to make it 17-0.

Mills' touchdown came on a third down. The 49ers struggled all game long, converting just 3 of 15 third-down attempts.

"I've been watching film hard all week. I've been studying that route. I just trusted my technique and trusted my feet and my safety over the top to jump the route," Mills said. "I jumped the route and picked the ball off."

"Any time you win a game in this league, it's a special thing. They're hard to come by. There are things that we talk about during the week like not having any letdowns," head coach Doug Pederson said after the win. "The guys really respond to that. Obviously, it pretty much rained the whole game. It's going

Eagles tight end Zak Ertz (86) pulls down one of his four receptions on the day. *AP Photo*

BOX SCORE

	1	2	3	4	T
San Francisco	0	0	7	3	10
Philadelphia	3	14	10	6	33

GAME LEADERS

PASSING YARDS
SF — C.J. Beathard 17-36, 167 YDS, 1 TD, 2 INT
PHI — C. Wentz 18-32, 211 YDS, 2 TD, 1 INT

RUSHING YARDS
SF — C.J. Beathard 6 CAR, 40 YDS
PHI — C. Clement 10 CAR, 54 YDS

RECEIVING YARDS
SF — M. Breida 4 REC, 39 YDS, 1 TD
PHI — A. Jeffery 2 REC, 62 YDS, 1 TD

to maybe knock you off just a little bit with the weather, but guys really responded, and did an outstanding job all game long. And to score 33 (points) like that, it was pretty impressive for them."

The lopsided score allowed coach Pederson to give Wentz the final six minutes off and let backup Nick Foles see his first action since returning to the Eagles. Foles led Philadelphia to the NFC East title in 2013 and was traded to the Rams in 2015. ∎

Eagles running back Corey Clement (30) makes the day of one lucky fan. *AP Photo*

EAGLES
BRONCOS

51
23

Nov. 5 vs. Denver   Lincoln Financial Field   Philadelphia, Pennsylvania

Eagles receiver Alshon Jeffery (17) scampers down the sideline for a 32-yard touchdown reception. *AP Photo*

Eagles Trounce Broncos

Carson Wentz isn't paying attention to his impressive stats.

Wentz tossed four touchdown passes, Corey Clement had three scores, and the Philadelphia Eagles routed the Denver Broncos 51-23 on Sunday.

The second-year quarterback leads the NFL with 23 TD passes, including 17 in the last five games.

"Touchdowns are great, but being 8-1 is what it's all about," Wentz said.

The Eagles dismantled the league's top-ranked defense, racking up 419 yards, to win their seventh straight game and head into a bye week with the best record in the league. Yet, Wentz sees room for improvement.

"Absolutely, we're never going to settle," he said. "Always things to learn from. I think we can keep getting better."

Brock Osweiler couldn't get the Broncos (3-5) on track in his first start since rejoining the team in September. He threw two interceptions.

"Every man has to do a self-check of himself," Broncos coach Vance Joseph said when asked if his team quit. "Only each man would know what his heart said to him in the fourth quarter. That's where I'll leave that."

Wentz was 15 of 27 for 199 yards before giving way to Nick Foles. He has three four-TD performances in the last five weeks.

"He improves every single week and the guys around him elevate their game," Eagles coach Doug Pederson said. "The great quarterbacks make the guys around them play at a higher level."

Clement had two TD runs and one TD catch, and newcomer Jay Ajayi ran for 77 yards and one score.

"Excited to be here," Ajayi said. "Great football town. Definitely believe we can do a lot of special things here."

Wentz flipped a 32-yard TD pass to Alshon Jeffery to give the Eagles a 7-3 lead after a holding penalty on Broncos cornerback Aqib Talib extended the drive. Talib bit on a faked inside handoff to Ajayi and Jeffery ran past him to make the catch and score.

After Osweiler threw a pick right to Patrick Robinson later in the first quarter, Wentz threw a short catch-and-run TD pass to Clement on third-and-10 from the 15.

A roughing-the-passer call on Denver's Zach Kerr kept another drive alive for Philadelphia.

Quarterback Carson Wentz threw for 199 yards and four touchdowns on the day. *AP Photo*

Wentz connected with Trey Burton on a 27-yard TD pass on the next play, giving the Eagles a 24-6 lead.

Ajayi burst through for a 46-yard TD run to put Philadelphia ahead 31-9 in the second quarter. Ajayi, a 2016 Pro Bowl pick with Miami, was acquired in a trade Tuesday. The

Broncos receiver Demaryius Thomas (88) is drilled by Eagles cornerback Patrick Robinson (21) after the catch.
AP Photo

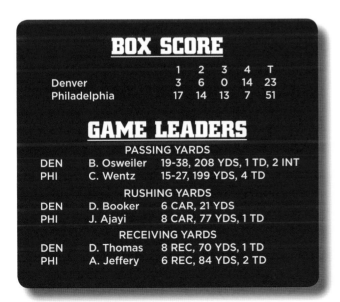

BOX SCORE

	1	2	3	4	T
Denver	3	6	0	14	23
Philadelphia	17	14	13	7	51

GAME LEADERS

PASSING YARDS
DEN	B. Osweiler	19-38, 208 YDS, 1 TD, 2 INT
PHI	C. Wentz	15-27, 199 YDS, 4 TD

RUSHING YARDS
DEN	D. Booker	6 CAR, 21 YDS
PHI	J. Ajayi	8 CAR, 77 YDS, 1 TD

RECEIVING YARDS
DEN	D. Thomas	8 REC, 70 YDS, 1 TD
PHI	A. Jeffery	6 REC, 84 YDS, 2 TD

Broncos hadn't allowed 30 points in a game this season, nor any TD runs.

Clement, an undrafted rookie free agent from Wisconsin, ran in from the 2 in the third quarter, and Wentz connected with Jeffery on a 6-yard pass to make it 44-9. Clement's 4-yard TD run capped the scoring.

The Eagles hadn't scored 50 points since a 54-11 victory over the Bears on Dec. 22, 2013.

"For us to be 8-1 right now, it's a tremendous credit to the guys and coaches in the locker room," Pederson said. "Hats off to those guys for the way they work, the way they practice, and prepare. And standing here looking back at it, I'm not surprised by the way they work." ∎

LINEBACKER
NIGEL BRADHAM

The Unsung Hero

Doug Pederson hadn't yet coached a game in Philadelphia when he was asked in July 2016 whether the team was going to release linebacker Nigel Bradham or not.

Bradham, whom the team signed in March that year, was arrested and charged with aggravated assault following an incident at the Hilton Bentley Miami in South Beach.

The Eagles stuck by him.

But a few months later, with the Eagles on a bye, Bradham, a Crawfordville, Fla., native, was arrested at Miami International Airport after TSA employees discovered a loaded handgun in his backpack.

The Eagles again stuck by him.

The patience has paid off.

Bradham, 28, has played some of the best football of his career in an Eagles uniform. The former Buffalo Bills linebacker started every game in 2016 and registered 102 combined tackles, two off a career-high.

When "MIKE" linebacker Jordan Hicks ruptured his Achilles in October, Bradham was forced into a leadership role, one he grabbed by the horns with the responsibility of wearing the radio communication in his helmet. In the game Hicks got hurt, on October 12 in Carolina, Bradham had one of the best games of his career.

In 15 regular season games, Bradham led the Eagles with 88 total tackles.

Bradham said he was appreciative that the Eagles stuck with him.

"It means everything, believing in me and my character and understanding me as a person and not just someone they didn't know," Bradham said Thursday. "They really treated me as family, and that's what that was. I felt that and it's grown.

"For us to be where we're at today, it's a blessing. There are reasons why that happened. Everything happens for a

Eagles outside linebacker Nigel Bradham (53) in action against the Los Angeles Rams. *AP Photo*

Nigel Bradham was the fourth-round draft pick of the Buffalo Bills in the 2012 NFL draft. *AP Photo*

reason. Whatever reason it was, it's definitely fortunate to have this journey that we're on. It's been an amazing ride. It's been up and down, but I wouldn't want it any other way."

Safety and team leader Malcolm Jenkins said Bradham's transition to the defensive signal caller went without issue.

"I've been on defenses where you lose your MIKE linebacker and things get crazy," Jenkins said. "They're not used to making calls, getting everybody lined up, communicating and also doing their job. But he's doing that and playing multiple positions, too. It's not like he just moved to the MIKE linebacker and that's it. He's MIKE in base, and all of a sudden, we go to dime packages and he's WILL.

"So he's having to learn all these different positions, take over that role of being the signal caller. But he's also our enforcer. He's the guy that we look for to get big hits, fly around, talk some trash and bring a little juice to the defense. A lot of times, that's hard to juggle all of that. He's really been kind of the unsung hero of our defense this year."

That "unsung hero" belief was shared by defensive coordinator Jim Schwartz earlier in the week.

"I think one of the unsung stories of this season has been Nigel picking up that communication," Schwartz said. "Nigel has always been a fiery guy. Sometimes I think he runs about five extra miles trying to get to the pile to make sure he's delivering whatever message he's going to deliver and it brings us a lot of energy, it really does.

"But that's a tough thing to do when you've got the coach speaking in your ear about, 'Hey, remind this guy this and we're going to this call, but check it to this if something else is going on'. And he's done a really good job handling all that communication, and it's been fairly seamless."

Bradham, who was Buffalo's fourth-round pick in 2012 after playing at Florida State, will be a free agent at year's end. Bradham said he'd like to remain an Eagle in the future.

"My style, my passion, and energy, everything fits well here," Bradham said. "We'll see." ▪

Eagles receiver Alshon Jeffery (17) makes an incredible diving catch on a 17-yard touchdown reception. *AP Photo*

EAGLES
COWBOYS

37
9

Nov. 19 vs. Dallas   AT&T Stadium   Arlington, Texas

Eagles running back Jay Ajayi (36) runs away from Dallas defenders Anthony Hitchens (59) and safety Byron Jones (31) on his way to a 71-yard gain. *AP Photo*

Hot Eagles Down Dallas

No kicker, no problem for the Philadelphia Eagles.

Carson Wentz threw for two touchdowns and three 2-point conversions after Philadelphia lost kicker Jake Elliott to a head injury, and the Eagles all but wrapped up the NFC East with a 37-9 victory over the Dallas Cowboys.

The Eagles (9-1) outscored the Cowboys 30-0 in the second half while extending their winning streak to eight games, their longest since 2003-04 and tied with New Orleans for the best current run in the NFL.

WORLD CHAMPIONS

Eagles linebacker Nigel Bradham (53) runs back a fumble recovery for a touchdown as teammate Chris Long (56) helps to clear his path. *AP Photo*

Eagles safety Malcolm Jenkins (27) and Cowboys wide receiver Dez Bryant (88) watch as the Eagles' Ronald Darby, top, intercepts a pass intended for Bryant. *AP Photo*

Philadelphia leads the second-place and defending division champion Cowboys (5-5) by four games with six to play after handing Dallas its worst home loss at 8-year-old AT&T Stadium.

Dallas' Dak Prescott threw a career-high three interceptions and lost a fumble that was returned for a touchdown in his second straight loss without star running back Ezekiel Elliott, serving a six-game suspension for alleged domestic violence.

Jake Elliott's injury wasn't a factor for nearly a half because the NFL-leading Eagles couldn't get in scoring position. They failed to get a first down on five straight first-half drives, starting with one at the Dallas 15 when Elliott missed a 34-yard attempt and soon after left the field.

Trailing 9-7 at halftime, Wentz led the Eagles on scoring drives of 75, 90 and 85 yards, the middle one boosted by Jay Ajayi's 71-yard run against his hometown team in his second game since getting traded by Miami.

"The biggest thing was sticking with the game plan," said Wentz, who is up to 25 touchdown passes with just five interceptions. "The big boys up front kind of came out angry. We ran the ball the second half really effectively."

At 9-1, the Eagles boast arguably one of the league's deepest and most dynamic set of running backs. It should come as no surprise that Pederson made the group the focal part of the game plan.

"We just wanted to commit back to the run. We didn't really change anything at halftime. We just committed to the same runs that we had," Eagles head coach Doug Pederson said. "We felt like we could just stay between the tackles and get some good double teams in there and the guys did a great job -- the offensive line, the tight ends, and the ball carriers breaking some tackles and making some good plays."

Ajayi had 91 yards on seven carries and LeGarrette Blount added 57 on 13 carries, including a 30-yarder leading to the last offensive touchdown.

Eagles quarterback Carson Wentz (11) passes to tight end Trey Burton (88) for a two point conversion. *AP Photo*

BOX SCORE

	1	2	3	4	T
Philadelphia	7	0	16	14	37
Dallas	6	3	0	0	9

GAME LEADERS

PASSING YARDS

PHI	C. Wentz	14-27, 168 YDS, 2 TD
DAL	D. Prescott	18-31, 145 YDS, 3 INT

RUSHING YARDS

PHI	J. Ajayi	7 CAR, 91 YDS
DAL	A. Morris	17 CAR, 91 YDS

RECEIVING YARDS

PHI	A. Jeffery	4 REC, 67 YDS, 1 TD
DAL	D. Bryant	8 REC, 63 YDS

Pederson declared at halftime that he would go for every fourth down and try 2-point conversions after every touchdown.

It came into play right away when Corey Clement scored on an 11-yard run to open the second half and ran in a screen pass behind three blockers for the 2-pointer.

The first fourth-down try was Wentz's 17-yard touchdown pass to Alshon Jeffery for a 29-9 lead. That 2-point pass failed. Torrey Smith had the other TD catch, an 11-yarder.

After Derek Barnett hit Prescott's leg and arm as he was throwing, Nigel Bradham picked up the loose ball and ran it 37 yards for a touchdown. Wentz's 2-point pass to Trey Burton provided the final margin.

"We got some nice 2-point conversions," said Wentz, who was 14 of 27 for 168 yards. "Now we've got to go back to the drawing board with our 2-point plays." ∎

Quarterback Carson Wentz (11) was 23-36 for 227 yards and three touchdowns. *AP Photo*

EAGLES
BEARS

31
3

Nov. 26 vs. Chicago   Lincoln Financial Field   Philadelphia, Pennsylvania

Eagles receiver Nelson Agholor (13) goes airborne as he reaches the end zone for a touchdown. *AP Photo*

Defense Dominant as Eagles
crush Bears

Another strong performance by Carson Wentz. Another dominant effort by the defense. Another lopsided win for the Philadelphia Eagles.

Wentz tossed three touchdown passes and the NFL-leading Eagles beat the Chicago Bears 31-3 Sunday for their ninth straight win.

The Eagles (10-1) reduced their magic number to clinch the NFC East to one with their fourth consecutive win by at least 23 points and third in a row by exactly 28. Philadelphia would secure its first division title since 2013 if the Cowboys (5-6) lose or tie Washington on Thursday night.

WORLD CHAMPIONS

"We're playing with a lot of momentum, a lot of energy, a lot of swagger," Wentz said.

Wentz had 227 yards passing, LeGarrette Blount ran for 97 yards and Zach Ertz caught 10 passes for 103 yards and one TD.

The defense shut down rookie quarterback Mitchell Trubisky and the inept Bears (3-8), holding them to zero first downs in the first half and 140 total yards in the game.

"That's the best defense I've ever played," Chicago offensive lineman Kyle Long said.

The Bears won the turnover battle (3-2), but couldn't do anything with excellent field position. They started consecutive drives at midfield and Philadelphia's 42 but Cairo Santos missed a 54-yard field goal.

"We didn't play well enough to compete," Bears coach John Fox said. "We needed to play really, really well in all three phases to beat that team."

Wentz threw a 17-yard TD pass to Ertz to give the Eagles a 7-0 lead on their second drive. Jay Ajayi ran 2 yards on fourth-and-1 to keep the drive going and Wentz connected with Alshon Jeffery for 14 yards on third-and-8 one play before the TD.

Wentz had a 15-yard TD pass to Nelson Agholor, who flipped over defenders into the end zone to make it 14-0 in the second quarter. Wentz spun away from a blitzer and ran 16 yards on third-and-9 to extend the drive. Then a holding penalty on Bears cornerback Prince Amukamara negated an incomplete pass on third-and-12, and the Eagles scored on the next play.

Another holding penalty on Amukamara gave the Eagles a first down late in the second quarter. Wentz then lofted an 8-yard TD pass

Eagles running back LaGarrette Blount (29) leaps over Bears defender Eddie Jackson (39) during the first half. *AP Photo*

to Jeffery to extend the lead to 24-0.

Ajayi ran 30 yards and fumbled at the Bears 5, but Agholor recovered in the end zone for a touchdown and a 31-3 lead.

"We're very balanced," Ajayi said. "We can do a lot of different things, so it keeps them on their toes."

Eagles wide receiver Alshon Jeffery (17) soars above the defense for a 8-yard touchdown reception with :05 seconds left in the first half. *AP Photo*

BOX SCORE

	1	2	3	4	T
Chicago	0	0	3	0	3
Philadelphia	7	17	0	7	31

GAME LEADERS

PASSING YARDS
CHI	M. Trubisky	17-33, 147 YDS, 2 INT
PHI	C. Wentz	23-36, 227 YDS, 3 TD

RUSHING YARDS
CHI	M. Trubisky	4 CAR, 12 YDS
PHI	L. Blount	15 CAR, 97 YDS

RECEIVING YARDS
CHI	D. Inman	4 REC, 64 YDS
PHI	Z. Ertz	10 REC, 103 YDS, 1 TD

The Bears entered with the fifth-ranked rushing offense and finished with 6 yards on 14 attempts. They had negative yards before Trubisky scrambled for 12 yards late in the fourth.

"It's really a pride issue when it comes to the run game," Eagles safety Malcolm Jenkins said. "Obviously, you have to be able to tackle as well. Our interior line is well-documented in what they can do. Our backers flow and hit, and when they do try to pack us all in and get to the edge, our corners show up with attitude. Knowing your scheme is a big deal, but a lot of the run game comes down to attitude." ∎

Seattle receiver Paul Richardson (10) is defended by Eagles cornerback Ronald Darby (41). *AP Photo*

SEAHAWKS 24
EAGLES 10

Dec. 3 vs. Seattle   CenturyLink Field   Seattle, Washington

Eagles quarterback Carson Wentz (11) fumbles the ball near the goal line as Seahawk defenders Earl Thomas (29) and Sheldon Richardson (91) close in. *AP Photo*

Too much Russell Wilson

Seahawks Edge Eagles

The Seahawks felt they were being written off, with injuries and the schedule converging to create doubt about whether Seattle was still among the NFC's elite.

With Russell Wilson, the Seahawks seemingly always have a chance.

"He was in the zone," Seattle wide receiver Doug Baldwin said. "I told him whatever that felt like, he's got to hold on to it because we need him to be in that mode for the rest of the season, because if he does that, we'll be unstoppable."

Wilson was masterful while throwing three touchdown passes, the last a 15-yard strike to J.D. McKissic with 7:29 left, and the Seahawks stayed in the NFC playoff hunt with a 24-10 victory over the Philadelphia Eagles.

Seattle (8-4) snapped Philadelphia's nine-game winning streak thanks largely to another brilliant performance by its quarterback. Wilson was 20 of 31 for 227 yards and threw touchdowns of 11 yards to Jimmy Graham, 1-yard to Tyler Lockettand the TD to McKissic after the Eagles had trimmed the lead to seven.

Philadelphia (10-2) was the highest-scoring team in the NFL with 31.9 points per game. But the Eagles got just 10 points out of seven drives that reached Seattle territory. Twice this year Seattle has faced what was the top scoring offense in the NFL at the time. Both times they scored 10 points against the Seahawks.

Carson Wentz was 29 of 45 for 348 yards with one touchdown and one interception. Wentz had a costly fumble at the Seattle 1 on the opening drive of the second half that could have pulled the Eagles even at 10-all.

Wentz was inches shy of breaking the plane when Sheldon Richardson ripped the ball free. The loose ball bounced around the end zone and eventually over the end line for a touchback and Seattle's ball. It was a major turning point, as Seattle went 80 yards in 11 plays, capped by Wilson's 1-yard pass to Lockett for a 17-3 Seattle lead.

"Fumbled, it happens. It's tough to do that on the road," Wentz said. "Situations like that, especially when you're down there on the 1-yard line, tough to do that and expect to win. Especially coming out the first drive of the second half, the way we did. We were rolling there. I just can't put it on the ground."

Seattle snapped a rare two-game losing streak at home mostly because of Wilson. It wasn't his best game in numbers, but it might be one of his best performances.

Eagles wide receiver Torrey Smith (82) celebrates with Nelson Agholor (13) after a touchdown. *AP Photo*

Seattle running back Mike Davis (39) is stopped short of the goal line by the Philadelphia defense during the second quarter. *AP Photo*

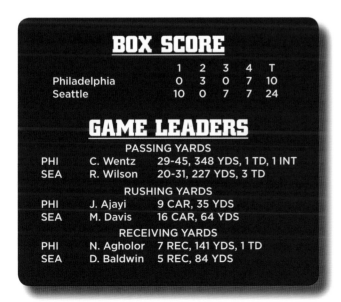

BOX SCORE

	1	2	3	4	T
Philadelphia	0	3	0	7	10
Seattle	10	0	7	7	24

GAME LEADERS

PASSING YARDS
PHI	C. Wentz	29-45, 348 YDS, 1 TD, 1 INT
SEA	R. Wilson	20-31, 227 YDS, 3 TD

RUSHING YARDS
PHI	J. Ajayi	9 CAR, 35 YDS
SEA	M. Davis	16 CAR, 64 YDS

RECEIVING YARDS
PHI	N. Agholor	7 REC, 141 YDS, 1 TD
SEA	D. Baldwin	5 REC, 84 YDS

"We had a good game plan going against (Wilson)," Philadelphia safety Corey Graham said. "But as you see, you know how it is, better in person than it is on film."

Wentz started a Philadelphia rally on the first play of the fourth quarter. Facing third-and-13 at the 16, Wentz was pressured from the pocket. As he was about to be dragged down by Quinton Jefferson, Wentz hit Nelson Agholor for 51 yards. Four plays later, and again facing third-and-long, Agholor beat Maxwell again and Wentz found him for a 27-yard TD to pull the Eagles within 17-10.

Agholor ended up with seven catches for 141 yards. ∎

DEFENSIVE TACKLE
FLETCHER COX

Man in the Middle

Fletcher Cox is playing in the first Super Bowl he's seeing.

Or so he says.

The three-time Pro Bowl defensive tackle is a big reason why the Philadelphia Eagles are facing the New England Patriots next Sunday in Minneapolis for a chance to bring home the franchise's first Vince Lombardi Trophy.

But the 27-year-old Cox isn't much of a football fan. He insists he's never even watched a Super Bowl.

"I don't watch sports," Cox said. "You know that."

If he spends the night getting in Tom Brady's face and helps the Eagles win their first NFL title since 1960, Cox may want to watch the highlights sometime.

First, all that matters is winning.

"We haven't been talked about all year," Cox said. "That's our story. No one has been talking about the Eagles, the defense, or the offense. If you go back and look, we finished in the top five of a bunch of different categories. This team just keeps finding ways to win, and that's our motto."

Cox, the 12th overall pick in the 2012 draft, had 5+ sacks in 14 games, recovered two fumbles and returned one for a touchdown. He often faces two or three blockers, so that allows his teammates opportunities to make plays.

"Cox is as good as anybody in the league at his position," Patriots coach Bill Belichick said. "He's a very disruptive player, hard to block, run, pass, no matter what it is."

Earning praise from Belichick doesn't come easy. Cox appreciates it.

"It's a lot of respect from a coach like Belichick, a guy that's been around, a guy that's seen a lot of great players in this league," he said. "For him to say that

Defensive tackle Fletcher Cox was the 12th overall pick in the 2012 NFL Draft. *AP Photo*

Cox has 5.5 sacks on the year while also being a dominant force against the run. *AP Photo*

that means I obviously must be doing something right. But at the same time, I've got three other guys besides me that's helping me push that limit, that's helping me get that recognition and I want to do the same thing for those guys."

The Eagles have plenty of depth on their defensive line. Ends Brandon Graham and Vinny Curry and tackle Tim Jernigan start along with Cox. Chris Long, Derek Barnett and Beau Allen also played at least 40 percent of the snaps.

"I wish it was just four (linemen)," Belichick said. "It's a very disruptive group. They have some edge rushers, a good interior pass rush. They come hard every play. You have to block them on every play. There are no plays off. To deal with that front down after down, they wear you down. It's a great group and a huge strength for their defense."

Defensive coordinator Jim Schwartz has enough confidence in all the players to rotate them in and out for series at a time. Because they split reps, they still look fresh this late in the season. It showed in a pair of dominant performances against the Falcons and Vikings in the playoffs.

"To roll in that many guys and not see a drop-off, it's great," Cox said. "We're pushing those guys to be on the same level as us."

Cox knows harassing Brady is the key to success against the Patriots. The Giants sacked Brady five times in their stunning Super Bowl upset 10 years ago, spoiling New England's perfect season.

Led by Cox and Graham, the Eagles generate a strong rush without having to blitz much. They'll need to keep extra defenders in the secondary against Brady.

"It's going to come down to the front four guys getting after the quarterback, making him uncomfortable in the pocket," Cox said.

Easier said than done against Brady. ∎

Eagles tight end Trey Burton (88) is able to hang on to a touchdown catch as Rams strong safety John Johnson tries to break up the play.
AP Photo

EAGLES
RAMS

43
35

Dec. 10 vs. Los Angeles   Los Angeles Memorial Coliseum   Los Angeles, California

Eagles quarterback Carson Wentz walks off the field after being injured during the second half. *AP Photo*

Eagles clinch NFC East

but lose Wentz

The Philadelphia Eagles might have lost star quarterback Carson Wentz for the rest of the season even as they clinched the NFC East title.

Wentz threw for 291 yards and four touchdowns before leaving with an injured left knee and Jake Elliott kicked the go-ahead 33-yard field goal with 3:45 left for the Eagles, who beat the Los Angeles Rams 43-35 in a thriller to clinch their first division title since 2013.

Eagles quarterback Carson Wentz (11) is tackled at the goal line during the second half. Wentz left the game shortly after the play and did not return. *AP Photo*

Two sources familiar with the injury said that doctors believe Wentz has torn his left anterior cruciate ligament and will miss the rest of the season and playoffs.

"I don't know anything yet until we evaluate him fully tomorrow," said coach Doug Pederson, adding that Wentz will have an MRI on Monday. "It's just a report. You're speculating that he's going to be out. I was really blocked on the play so I've got to check out the tape tonight on the way home. I knew something was up but didn't know the extent of it, obviously."

Wentz was hit hard as he dove into the end zone on a play that was called back because of holding. He stayed in the game and threw a 3-yard touchdown pass to Alshon Jeffery four plays later to give the Eagles a 31-28 lead.

Nick Foles replaced Wentz on the next drive for Philadelphia (11-2).

"I just saw him favoring his leg a little bit and it's just one of those things where he toughed it out, threw a touchdown," Foles said. "He's one of the toughest players I've played with. He came to the side and got checked and I was told be ready to go in."

Foles said Wentz was waiting for the team when it came into the locker room after the game.

"The guy's really rallied. It means a lot to this team, it means a lot to me. Excited we're NFC East champs but it's emotional, a guy you work with every day who you think the world of, you know I think he's the MVP; it's not easy but I know this team will step up and rally no matter what."

Carson Wentz (11), LaGarrette Blount (29), and Trey Burton (88) help Brent Celek (87) celebrate his first quarter touchdown catch. *AP Photo*

BOX SCORE

	1	2	3	4	T
Philadelphia	14	10	7	12	43
Los Angeles	7	7	14	7	35

GAME LEADERS

PASSING YARDS
PHI	C. Wentz	23-41, 291 YDS, 4 TD, 1 INT
LAR	J. Goff	16-26, 199 YDS, 2 TD

RUSHING YARDS
PHI	J. Ajayi	15 CAR, 78 YDS
LAR	T. Gurley II	13 CAR, 96 YDS, 2 TD

RECEIVING YARDS
PHI	T. Smith	6 REC, 100 YDS
LAR	C. Kupp	5 REC, 118 YDS, 1 TD

The NFC West-leading Rams (9-4) then went up 35-31 on Todd Gurley's second short TD run.

Elliott kicked a 41-yard field goal to pull the Eagles to 35-34. His go-ahead field goal was set up when Chris Long, a second-round draft pick of the then-St. Louis Rams in 2008, had a strip-sack of Jared Goff, with Rodney McLeod recovering.

Seeing Wentz go out didn't change the Rams' thoughts on their chances to win.

"There was still the whole fourth quarter left, and Nick's no slouch himself," Goff said. "He's played in the league for a long time and can do some things and clearly showed that tonight."

The game ended on a crazy play, when Philadelphia's Brandon Graham grabbed a lateral by Tavon Austin out of the air and scored what was ruled a 16-yard fumble return. ∎

WORLD CHAMPIONS

71

Eagles receiver Nelson Agholor (13) hangs on to the touchdown catch as Giants defensive back Darryl Morris (23) defends. *AP Photo*

EAGLES
GIANTS

34
29

REGULAR
SEASON
GAME

Dec. 17 vs. New York   MetLife Stadium   East Rutherford, New Jersey

Eagles quarterback Nick Foles (9) tosses one of four touchdown passes against New York. *AP Photo*

Foles throws four TDs

in first start

WORLD CHAMPIONS

Nick Foles replaced the injured Carson Wentz, and nothing really changed for the Philadelphia Eagles.

They got four touchdown passes from their quarterback, like they did a week ago, and won again to secure a first-round playoff bye.

Another ho-hum day for the best team in the NFC.

Foles hit four different receivers on touchdown passes ranging from 3 to 13 yards in his first start, and the Eagles (12-2) rallied from an early 14-point deficit to defeat the surprising New York Giants 34-29.

"I thought he played well," Eagles coach Doug Pederson said of Foles. "There are some things he would like to do over. Every

Eagles outside linebacker Kamu Grugier-Hill, right, blocks a punt from Giants punter Brad Wing, left. *AP Photo*

game is going be that way. I thought he handled himself extremely well, a lot of poise. He did a nice job."

There was speculation the Eagles would rely on their running game this week against the Giants (2-12) to give Foles time to adjust to the offense. Pederson ruled that out.

"With him coming out and saying he's not changing anything, it says a lot about his confidence in me and his confidence in the players in the offense," said Foles, who completed 24 of 38 passes for 237 yards and no interceptions.

Foles clearly is no Wentz. He is more a pocket passer, and there were times in the game when Wentz clearly would have been scrambling for a first down. Foles carried twice for zero yards. But like Wentz, Foles was efficient in the red zone as all of Philadelphia's touchdowns came inside the Giants' 20. He also placed an emphasis on spreading the ball around connecting with seven different

receivers on the afternoon.

"He was definitely sending me texts before the game. I haven't had a chance to look at my phone but just wishing us luck," Foles said when asked if Wentz spoke to him before the game. "Going out there and getting this win, I know he's really excited."

The Eagles made a late stand on first-and-goal in the final minute in edging the Giants for the second time this season, spoiling a three-touchdown, season-high 434-yard passing game by Eli Manning.

Foles hit Alshon Jeffery, Zach Ertz, Trey Burton and Nelson Agholor on scoring passes in filling in for Wentz, who tore an ACL last week and was lost for the season after a brilliant year.

The Eagles also got two field goals from Jake Elliott and three blocked kicks from their special teams, foiling an extra point, a punt and field goal. The block on the punt set up a touchdown.

Giants quarterback Eli Manning (10) is sacked by Eagles defensive end Brandon Graham (55) during first half action. *AP Photo*

BOX SCORE

	1	2	3	4	T
Philadelphia	7	14	10	3	34
New York	13	10	6	0	29

GAME LEADERS

PASSING YARDS

PHI	N. Foles	24-38, 237 YDS, 4 TD
NYG	E. Manning	37-57, 434 YDS, 3 TD, 1 INT

RUSHING YARDS

PHI	J. Ajayi	12 CAR, 49 YDS
NYG	W. Gallman	8 CAR, 39 YDS

RECEIVING YARDS

PHI	N. Agholor	7 REC, 59 YDS, 1 TD
NYG	S. Shepard	11 REC, 139 YDS, 1 TD

"We had to make up for what happened last week," said Kamu Grugier-Hill, who blocked a Brad Wing punt late in the first half to give the Eagles the football at New York's 20-yard line. The Eagles scored a touchdown three plays later to take a 21-20 lead, erasing a 13-point deficit. "Making a difference on special teams is something we pride ourselves on. This team has been doing it the last three or four years, so going out there today and blocking kicks and helping us win, that's what the special teams are all about."

Philadelphia will play its final two regular-season game at home and then wait for the conference semifinal.

"It's obviously something great," Foles said of the bye. "I was fortunate to be a part of it last year in Kansas City. We still have a lot of work to do this season. The big thing is you let your body recover." ▪

Eagles cornerback Jalen Mills (31) breaks up a pass intended for Raiders receiver Michael Crabtree (15). *AP Photo*

EAGLES
RAIDERS

19
10

Dec. 25 vs. Oakland   **Lincoln Financial Field**   **Philadelphia, Pennsylvania**

Eagles defensive end Derek Barnett (96) returns a fumble 23-yards for a touchdown late in the fourth quarter. *AP Photo*

Eagles clinch No. 1 seed with

19-10 win over Raiders

The road to the Super Bowl in the NFC goes through Philadelphia.

Jake Elliott kicked a 48-yard field goal with 22 seconds left, and the Eagles clinched the No. 1 seed for the NFC playoffs with a sloppy 19-10 victory over the Oakland Raiders on Monday night.

The Eagles (13-2) went to the Super Bowl and lost 24-21 to New England the last time they had home-field advantage following the 2004 season.

They'll need the edge after a second straight poor performance. The defense struggled in a 34-29 win at the Giants last week. The offense was awful against the Raiders.

WORLD CHAMPIONS

Eagles running back Jay Ajayi (36) makes the reception and scampers 17-yards for a touchdown. *AP Photo*

"We played great team ball," cornerback Patrick Robinson said. "The offense didn't play as well as they have been, the defense had to step up."

Ronald Darby intercepted Derek Carr's pass and ran it back 52 yards with 54 seconds left, but was ruled down by contact at the spot of the pick. Nick Foles then completed four straight passes for 21 yards. After an incomplete pass, Elliott nailed his kick right down the middle.

"We have to pick up for each other," Darby said.

Derek Barnett returned a fumble 23 yards for a touchdown after picking up a lateral on Oakland's final play from scrimmage.

"I thought the defense played really, really well," head coach Doug Pederson said. "They kept us in the football game, special teams. (It was a) team effort, though. (We) found a way, sitting here today at 13-2. Everybody's got to come through here now. That's the exciting part."

Making his second start since MVP candidate Carson Wentz tore his left ACL, Foles had a tough time on a windy night. He was 19 of 38 for 163 yards with one TD and one interception.

"I didn't play good enough," Foles said. "I have to play cleaner, (need) pinpoint accuracy and good decisions on third downs."

Carr was even worse. He was 15 of 29 for 140 yards, one TD and two interceptions.

Carr threw a 63-yard TD pass to Amari Cooper to tie it at 7 early in the second quarter. Cooper was wide open after cornerback Jalen Mills tried to jump the route.

Giorgio Tavecchio kicked a 25-yard field goal on the opening drive of the third quarter to give the Raiders a 10-7 lead.

The teams traded turnovers on three straight possessions, starting with Robinson intercepting Carr and returning it to Oakland's 44.

Eagles left guard Chance Warmack then caused Jay Ajayi to fumble when he tried to

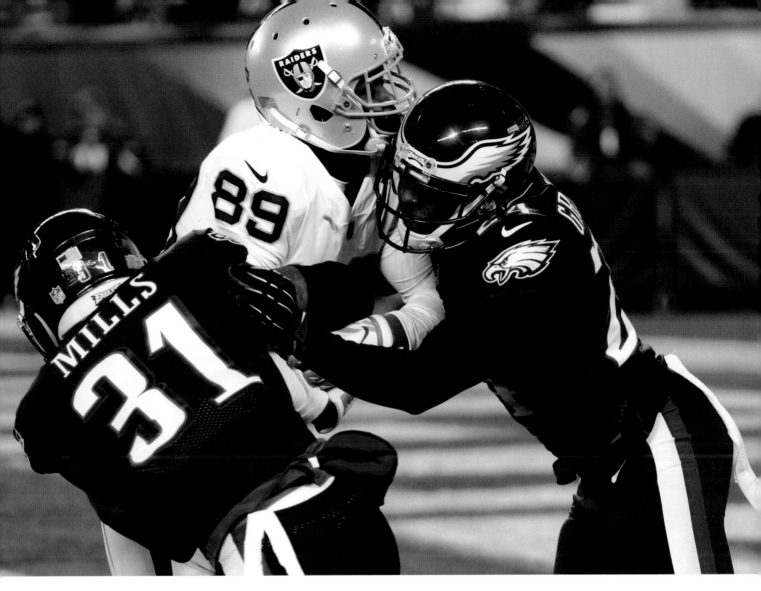

Raiders receiver Amari Cooper (89) is wrapped up by Eagles defenders Jalen Mills (31) and Corey Graham (24). *AP Photo*

BOX SCORE

	1	2	3	4	T
Oakland	0	7	3	0	10
Philadelphia	7	0	3	9	19

GAME LEADERS

PASSING YARDS
OAK	D. Carr	15-29, 140 YDS, 1 TD, 2 INT
PHI	N. Foles	19-38, 163 YDS, 1 TD, 1 INT

RUSHING YARDS
OAK	M. Lynch	25 CAR, 95 YDS
PHI	J. Ajayi	14 CAR, 52 YDS

RECEIVING YARDS
OAK	A. Cooper	3 REC, 66 YDS, 1 TD
PHI	Z. Ertz	9 REC, 81 YDS

push the pile and hit his teammate. The Raiders recovered at their 30, but gave it back on the next play when Marshawn Lynch fumbled at the same spot.

Philadelphia couldn't do much with excellent field position and settled for Elliott's tying 35-yard field goal.

After Tavecchio missed a 48-yard field goal with 7:58 remaining, Foles threw a pass that bounced off Pro Bowl tight end Zach Ertz's hands and was intercepted by Reggie Nelson at the Eagles 37.

But Philadelphia quickly got the ball back when Malcolm Jenkins stripped Jalen Richard and recovered it at the Eagles 16. The offense went three-and-out.

Oakland's first drive ended with Carr throwing the ball away on fourth-and-2 from Philadelphia's 42.

The Eagles scored on the ensuing possession when Foles tossed a 17-yard TD pass to Ajayi for a 7-0 lead. Corey Clement ran 2 yards on fourth-and-1 to extend the drive. ∎

QUARTERBACK NICK FOLES

Foles goes from nearly retiring to Super Bowl debut

Not long ago Nick Foles contemplated retiring from the NFL after losing his passion for football but now the Philadelphia Eagles quarterback is flying high ahead of his first Super Bowl.

The 29-year-old Foles had such a difficult and unfulfilling 2015 season with the St. Louis Rams that he seriously wondered whether there was any reason to keep playing in the league.

"Once I was a free agent it was just an opportunity to sit there and in my heart at the time I was probably going to step away from the game," Foles recalled. "But I also knew just being in that situation that I needed to take a few days just to let all the emotions settle."

Taking some time before making his decision has paid off as Foles will now lead his Eagles into a Super Bowl clash against the New England Patriots in Minneapolis.

Foles was drafted by Philadelphia in 2012 and tabbed as the team's quarterback of the future but an inconsistent rookie year meant he started the 2013 season as Michael Vick's backup. But injuries to Vick gave Foles another shot, only this time he did not let it go to waste and proved to be the driving force behind the Eagles' second-half surge to the playoffs.

The Eagles, however, decided to end the Foles experiment in 2015 when they traded him to St. Louis, which put in motion what nearly spelled the end of his career.

Foles played one forgettable campaign with the Rams before the disgruntled signal caller skipped offseason workouts after the team selected quarterback Jared Goff with the first overall draft pick. He eventually asked to be released and decided to go on a fly-fishing camping trip with his brother-in-law, discussed options with his wife and, when he still did not have a clear decision of what to do, turned to prayer.

"At that point there were several teams that called but the only one I was going to play for was Kansas City because of coach (Andy) Reid

Foles fires a pass in the Eagles divisional playoff win over Atlanta. *AP Photo*

Quarterback Nick Foles barks out the signals prior to the snap in a late season win against the NY Giants. *AP Photo*

being there," Foles said of his former Eagles coach.

"He's a man that has always believed in me, no matter what has gone on in my career. He drafted me. I knew that if I went and played with him I would give it one more shot that he could find the joy. If I had joy in there he could bring it back out and he sure did."

Foles filled in admirably as the Chiefs backup and while his stay there lasted only one season he said it was a big reason why he is where he is today.

"Being in Kansas City last year was one of the very special years of my football career," said Foles.

"Very grateful for the opportunity that he (Reid) gave me and the belief he's always shown me. I am sitting here today and I might not be here if I didn't have coach Reid right there so I am glad he took me in."

When the Eagles came calling, in pursuit of a back-up for The Franchise, Carson Wentz, Foles knew he wasn't signing to start. He wound up doing so anyway.

After 13 regular season weeks of watching Wentz become the city's star, Foles was called into action against the LA Rams and soon became the default starter for a Super Bowl contender.

He struggled at first, and fans yearned for Nate Sudfeld, an unproven, undrafted practice squad player. Eagles coach Doug Pederson never wavered on his support for Foles, and his teammates rallied around him.

He's made them proud.

Foles was solid in the NFC Divisional round against the Atlanta Falcons, and stellar in the NFC Championship game against the Minnesota Vikings. He has completed 77 percent of his passes in the playoffs for 598 yards, three touchdowns and no interceptions.

"He's a great player," said Eagles receiver Nelson Agholor. "We've got a great coaching staff but respect has to be given to Nick. Nick is a great player who has proven himself in this league. He's a Pro Bowler. We know he's going to go out there, grind and prepare to finish the job." ∎

Dallas Cowboys defensive end Datone Jones (56) blocks a pass from Eagles quarterback Nate Sudfeld (7). *AP Photo*

COWBOYS
EAGLES

6
0

Dec. 31 vs. Dallas   Lincoln Financial Field   Philadelphia, Pennsylvania

Cowboys running back Ezekiel Elliott (21) reaches for the ball after a botched handoff as Eagles defenders Destiny Vaeao (97) and Vinny Curry (75) close in. *AP Photo*

Cowboys sneak past playoff-bound Eagles

Healthy? Yes. Sharp? Not quite.

The Philadelphia Eagles are heading into the playoffs with no further injuries after playing it safe in a 6-0 loss to Dallas on Sunday.

Dak Prescott tossed a 20-yard touchdown pass to Brice Butler early in the fourth quarter and the Cowboys denied the Eagles a franchise-record 14th win.

The Eagles (13-3) rested several starters on a frigid day and played others briefly after securing the NFC's No. 1 seed last week. They'll have two weeks to work on a slumping offense before hosting a playoff game on Jan. 13 or 14.

Cowboys tight end James Hanna (84) is de-cleated by Eagles cornerback Rasul Douglas (32). *AP Photo*

"I'm not concerned," Eagles head coach Doug Pederson said. "I have confidence in our guys."

Nick Foles struggled in one quarter, going 4 of 11 for 39 yards with one interception. Foles was excellent in his first start after Carson Wentz went down for the season, tossing four TD passes in a 34-29 win at the Giants on Dec. 17. But he has followed up with two poor performances.

"I feel great and I know what I can do," Foles said. "I know the guys are confident in me. We expect to execute better. This wasn't acceptable. We know how talented we can be. We can do special stuff."

Second-year pro Nate Sudfeld replaced Foles and was 19 of 23 for 134 yards in his first career game. He was tackled inside the 5 after catching a lateral on a desperation play to end the game.

"Pretty solid for the most part in terms of efficiency and everything," Sudfeld said. "But I felt there were some plays that we weren't able to finish."

The Cowboys (9-7) earned their second straight winning season for the first time since five in a row from 2005-09. That's little consolation for Dallas, which was eliminated from playoff contention in Week 16.

"I'm sad the season is over," Ezekiel Elliott said. "I wish we were playing in the playoffs. I'm going to use that as fuel for next year."

The Cowboys drove 99 yards for the first score. A holding penalty on Rasul Douglas on an incomplete pass on third down extended the drive and Prescott connected with Butler on a slant on third-and-7. Dan Bailey hooked the extra point wide left, only his second career miss in 278 tries.

Bailey also missed a 23-yard field goal wide left with 13 seconds remaining.

The teams were 0 for 12 on third and fourth

Cowboys quarterback Zak Prescott (4) is sandwiched by Eagles defensive end Steven Means (51). *AP Photo*

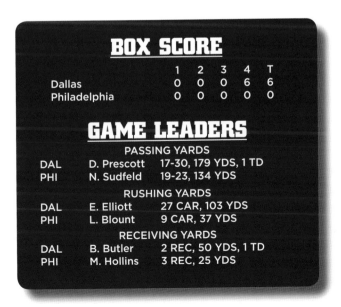

BOX SCORE

	1	2	3	4	T
Dallas	0	0	0	6	6
Philadelphia	0	0	0	0	0

GAME LEADERS

PASSING YARDS
DAL	D. Prescott	17-30, 179 YDS, 1 TD
PHI	N. Sudfeld	19-23, 134 YDS

RUSHING YARDS
DAL	E. Elliott	27 CAR, 103 YDS
PHI	L. Blount	9 CAR, 37 YDS

RECEIVING YARDS
DAL	B. Butler	2 REC, 50 YDS, 1 TD
PHI	M. Hollins	3 REC, 25 YDS

down before the Cowboys converted on third down late in the second quarter. The Eagles got their first third-down conversion midway through the third quarter. Sudfeld then ran 22 yards on another third down and the crowd roared.

Philadelphia's best drive with Foles was the game opener. The Eagles drove to the Cowboys 39 before Torrey Smith dropped a pass on third-and-7. Foles was hurried and threw an incomplete pass on fourth down.

Foles underthrew Alshon Jeffery and was picked by Chidobe Awuzie at the Cowboys 48 on Philadelphia's third possession. It was Awuzie's first career interception. The offense went three-and-out on the first unit's fourth and final series. ∎

COACH DOUG PEDERSON

The Genuine Article

Doug Pederson is one win away from bringing Philadelphia the elusive Super Bowl title his mentor couldn't deliver.

If the Eagles (15-3) beat New England (15-3) on Sunday, Pederson will hoist the Vince Lombardi Trophy and Philadelphia will celebrate its first NFL title since beating Lombardi's Green Bay Packers in 1960.

No one saw this coming two years ago.

After abruptly firing Chip Kelly, Eagles owner Jeffery Lurie longed for a coach more like the one he used to have: Andy Reid. Even though Reid failed to win the big game during his 14-year tenure in Philadelphia, he won more games than any coach in franchise history and led the Eagles to nine playoff appearances, five NFC title games and a Super Bowl loss to the Patriots.

Reid also had a close relationship with Lurie, was well-liked by the players and instilled a family atmosphere. That culture was an important element for Lurie. The environment had changed under Kelly, who was 26-21 in three seasons. Though he was an innovative coach, Kelly didn't connect well with all his players and members of the organization.

So Lurie went back to what he knew and hired Pederson, Reid's protégé.

Lurie was quite familiar with Pederson, who was a quarterback for Reid with the Eagles in 1999 and then an assistant coach on his staff in Philadelphia and Kansas City.

Other coaches had more impressive resumes, but Lurie liked Pederson's intangibles.

"I spent a lot of time with players at the end of that (2015) season and I thought what was really needed was a kind of leadership that leads with a genuineness, a real genuineness," Lurie said. "And people laughed when I used the term

Head coach Doug Pederson looks over his play chart during a recent game. *AP Photo*

Pederson, a former NFL quarterback, tosses the ball around before a practice at the team's training facility. *AP Photo*

'emotional intelligence,' but that's probably a really good way to describe it.

"There's a lot of great coaches. They all have their different styles, but the one common ground among them all is absolute consistency and genuineness. And Doug Pederson is just himself. And at times that's very humble, and at times it's just very real. At times that's very bright. At times it's tough. But he does it in a true, genuine way and I think players really respond to that in today's world."

Naturally, Pederson learned from Reid.

"Being around him, he's the same day in and day out," Pederson said. "Same consistency. Same work ethic."

Like Reid, Pederson had his share of critics. He wasn't the people's choice in Philly when he got the job and ESPN ranked him the worst hire of his coaching class at the time. Three of the six other coaches already have been fired.

"I don't pay any attention to that, quite honestly," Pederson said. "I drive home at night knowing I put in a full day's work. I get up in the morning to come in here, and however I can serve this organization and serve these players, that's all I know."

Pederson cares about his players, improving their game and making them better men off the field.

"Coach Pederson is an unbelievable coach to play for," said Nick Foles, who went from backup quarterback to hero of the NFC championship game. "He just has such a great feel for the game.

"I played for some amazing coaches, and Doug is an unbelievable play caller," Foles said. "The attention to detail is unbelievable and we go into a game feeling 100 percent confident in the game plan. That's big for an athlete when you can go out there and trust everything." ∎

Falcons receiver Julio Jones can't make the catch on a fourth down pass in the end zone as Eagles cornerback Jalen Mills defends. *AP Photo*

EAGLES
FALCONS

15
10

NFC
DIVISIONAL
PLAYOFF

Jan. 13 vs. Atlanta   Lincoln Financial Field   Philadelphia, Pennsylvania

Eagles defenders Brandon Graham (55) and Jalen Mills (31) celebrate after Falcons receiver Julio Jones (11) can't make a fourth down catch in the end zone. *AP Photo*

Underdog Eagles goal-line stand

sends Falcons packing

Fly Eagles Fly.

With the wind and against it.

With Nick Foles engineering several long drives, Jake Elliott converting three field goals, and the defense getting stingy in the tightest spot, Philadelphia moved into the NFC championship game with a 15-10 victory over the Atlanta Falcons.

Foles directed brilliant marches of 74 and 80 yards in the second half - one into the whipping wind, the other with it - and Elliott atoned for missing an extra point by converting from 53 yards at the end of the

WORLD CHAMPIONS

89

Eagles running back LaGarrette Blount (29) scores on a 1-yard run in the second quarter. *AP Photo*

second quarter, and 37 and 21 in the second half. Then the Eagles (14-3) held when Atlanta (11-7) got to the 9-yard line with a first down, and to the 2 on fourth down.

When Matt Ryan's final pass sailed over Julio Jones' head in the end zone, Philly could celebrate its first playoff victory since the 2008 season.

"I mean, we just kept believing in each other," said Foles, who became the starter when Carson Wentz, a leading MVP contender, injured his knee in December. "That was it. Our team never wavered, defense did an amazing job, special teams - that's just been the story this year is that we just all stuck together..."

The Falcons, of course, memorably blew a 28-3 second-half lead to the Patriots in last year's Super Bowl. They will not get the opportunity to atone for it, though Ryan got them close at the end.

Despite being underdogs as the No. 1 seed, the Eagles showed plenty of moxie.

"Just keep on disrespecting and we're going to keep proving people wrong," receiver Alshon Jeffery said.

Mistakes hurt the Eagles in the opening half. Jay Ajayi's fumble and a misplayed punt that bounced off Bryan Braman led to all 10 Atlanta points.

Things began nicely for Philadelphia when

Eagles kicker Jake Elliott drills a 53-yard field goal on the last play of the first half. *AP Photo*

Falcons receiver Mohamed Sanu (12) can't hang on to the pass after taking a hit from Eagles safety Rodney McLeod (23). *AP Photo*

safety Brian Poole was tagged with pass interference on a deep pass by Foles that was held up by the wind. But Ajayi fumbled on the next play with Keanu Neal recovering.

Atlanta efficiently mixed runs and passes on their next drive resulting in Matt Bryant's 33-yard field goal for an early 3-0 lead.

Philadelphia got the run game going with Ajayi in the opening period. Then, with the wind in the next quarter, the Eagles kept the Falcons so off-balance Atlanta took two timeouts in three plays.

Receiver Nelson Agholor's 21-yard run got the ball to the 3, but Foles botched a handoff to Corey Clement. But the quarterback quickly dived on the loose ball and was ruled to have scored. Replay showed otherwise.

Pederson showed no hesitation going for it, and Blount surged in from the 1. Elliott's missed extra point left it 6-3.

Soon after came Matt Bosher's punt that took a wicked bounce and hit Braman while he was blocking. From the Philly 18, the Falcons benefited from two penalties before Ryan scrambled from pressure and found Devonta Freeman for a 6-yard TD and a 10-3 lead.

With 46 seconds left in the half, the hosts got lucky. Foles' errant pass ricocheted off Neal's hands to Torrey Smith for 20 yards. Jeffery made a long stretch to haul in another throw with 1 second remaining, and Elliott's 53-yard field goal just made it over the crossbar.

"It was great for momentum," Foles said.

"Jake did an awesome job of kicking that for us."

A masterful 74-yard, 12-play drive on which Foles threw for 70 yards led to Elliott's 37-yard kick into the wind that made it 12-10. The Eagles then put together their best drive, an 80-yarder covering 14 plays, but yet again faltered close to the end zone. Elliott added a 21-yarder with 6:02 remaining after head coach Doug Pederson briefly considered going for it

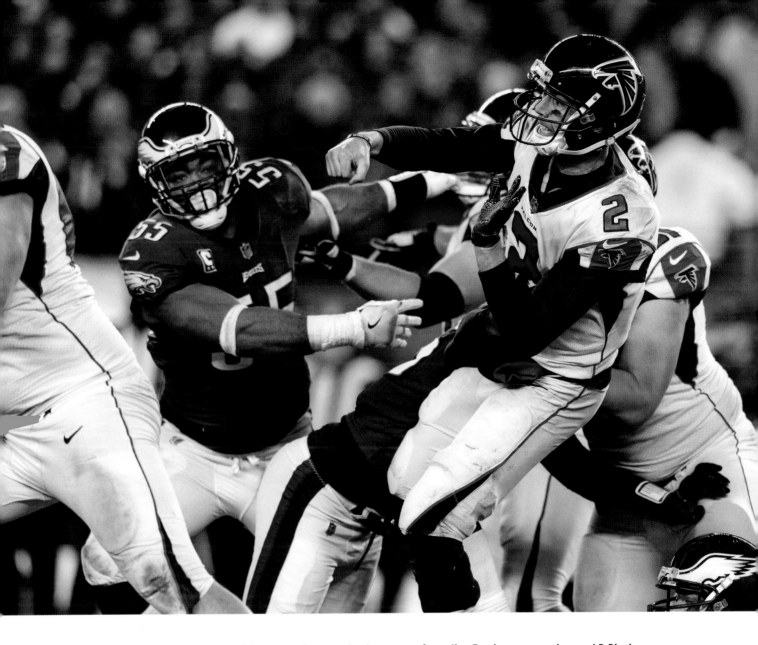

Falcons quarterback Matt Ryan (2) was under constant pressure from the Eagles pass rushers. *AP Photo*

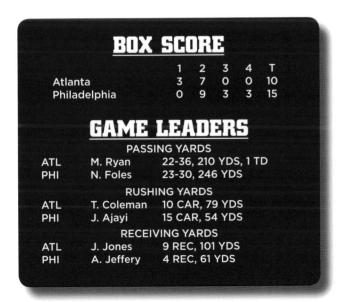

BOX SCORE

	1	2	3	4	T
Atlanta	3	7	0	0	10
Philadelphia	0	9	3	3	15

GAME LEADERS

PASSING YARDS
ATL	M. Ryan	22-36, 210 YDS, 1 TD
PHI	N. Foles	23-30, 246 YDS

RUSHING YARDS
ATL	T. Coleman	10 CAR, 79 YDS
PHI	J. Ajayi	15 CAR, 54 YDS

RECEIVING YARDS
ATL	J. Jones	9 REC, 101 YDS
PHI	A. Jeffery	4 REC, 61 YDS

on fourth-and-1 at the Atlanta 3.

"It was tricky out there, really gusty," Elliott said.

While the fans in the Linc held their breath, the Eagles defense held deep in their own territory on the Falcons last drive.

"Man, just stay calm," said defensive tackle Fletcher Cox, who was a force all day. "We always talk about that. We've been in those situations during the regular season, so we kind of know how to handle those situations, not try to make a play but let the play come to us."

And the road to the Super Bowl remains through Philly. ∎

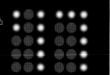
THE ARCHITECT

Roseman built Eagles for Super Bowl moment

No matter how the change of Howie Roseman's job duties in 2015 was framed, with a new fancy vice president title and a reassignment of duties, there was no question he was the loser in a power struggle with former head coach Chip Kelly.

And yet now Roseman looks back at his year in Eagles exile, where he focused on business operations and had no role in building the roster, as a "great experience" that ultimately helped him when he regained personnel power after Kelly was fired at the end of that season.

It was a chance to reflect on his career after a rapid rise through the Eagles' personnel ranks, and a chance to see a different side of how an NFL franchise runs.

"When you have a year where you're away from the daily grind of what you're doing, you have a chance to think differently about your relationships or what you're doing on a daily basis," Roseman said.

In the two years Roseman has been back in charge of the Eagles, he's made bold moves that have turned Philadelphia into an NFC champion positioned for sustained success.

The Eagles have 20 projected starters under contract for 2018, like quarterback Carson Wentz, left tackle Jason Peters and linebacker Jordan Hicks, who all will miss the Super Bowl because of injuries

"Make sure that you're not short-changing what the right way to build the team is, and what you believe in," Roseman said. "Even if that means taking one step back in order to take two steps forward."

It started with a clear plan in 2016 to acquire a franchise quarterback, a vision Roseman laid out for Doug Pederson upon the head coach's arrival that January.

The Eagles traded five draft picks to the Cleveland Browns to move up from No. 8 to No. 2 to draft Wentz. Before last season began, Roseman unloaded former starter Sam Bradford to the Vikings, receiving a first-round pick in return.

Eagles players said that the decision to sign Nick Foles, a former Eagles draft pick (by Andy Reid) and starter (under Kelly) to a two-year deal with $7 million guaranteed was a critical decision that helped keep the Eagles afloat after Wentz' injury.

"Obviously when you hit with a franchise quarterback like Carson, that's so big for a team," said center Jason Kelce. "But they went and got Nick Foles for a reason and it's paid off for us. Not too many teams are fortunate enough to have a backup quarterback be able to go in there and still lead them to a Super Bowl."

The Foles deal was one of several seemingly small-scale moves from the 2017 offseason made by Roseman. He boosted an underwhelming receiving corps by landing Alshon Jeffery and Torrey Smith in free agency and added veterans to bolster the defensive line and secondary.

"It was about building the talent around (Wentz). And it's not just offensive guys, it's also acquiring talent on defense," Pederson said. "You have to do that. You've got to be able to have those guys around your quarterback."

Yet for all the building he's done, Roseman made waves by quickly trading away many of Kelly's signature signigns, like running back DeMarco Murray (dispatched to the Titans), cornerback Byron Maxwell and linebacker Kiko Alonso (both sent to the Dolphins).

But he's also brought on talent via trades, including cornerback Ronald Darby (acquired from the Bills for a third rounder and former Kelly draft pick receiver Jordan Matthews), and running back Jay Ajayi (obtained from the Dolphins in November for a fourth-round selection).

To veteran Eagles players, who were around for Roseman's earlier years as general manager and stuck around after Kelly's tenure, the recent moves made a particularly strong impression.

"Howie knows what direction he wanted to take the team and hats off to him, because look where we're at right now," Eagles defensive end Vinny Curry said. "I feel like he doesn't get enough credit that he deserves." ∎

Howie Roseman, Philadelphia Eagles executive vice president of football operations, lifts the NFC championship trophy after the Eagles' 38-7 win over the Minnesota Vikings.
AP Photo

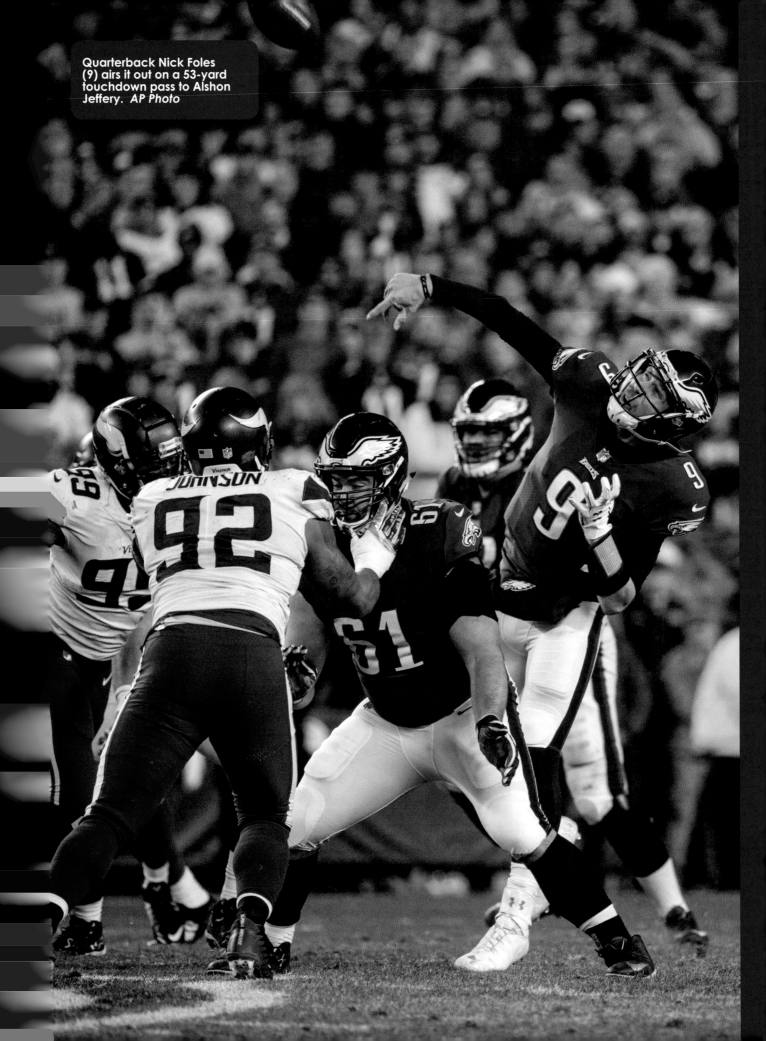

Quarterback Nick Foles (9) airs it out on a 53-yard touchdown pass to Alshon Jeffery. *AP Photo*

EAGLES
VIKINGS

38
7

Jan. 21 vs. Minnesota   Lincoln Financial Field   Philadelphia, Pennsylvania

Team owner Jeffery Lurie and the Philadelphia Eagles celebrate with the George Halas Trophy after winning the NFC Championship. *AP Photo*

Eagles Fly into Super Bowl

With one quarter remaining, Eagles players on the field and sideline already were dancing.

A bit later, after their stunning and resounding 38-7 rout of the Minnesota Vikings earned them the NFC championship, they listened as nearly 70,000 made the Linc shake with "Fly Eagles Fly."

Hey Philly, you're in the Super Bowl.

"It was electric. The fans are awesome," All-Pro tackle Lane Johnson said.

"We're going there to prove we belong," added Brandon Graham of the meeting with the AFC

Eagles cornerback Patrick Robinson (21) eludes numerous Vikings players as he returns an interception 50-yards for a touchdown. *AP Photo*

Eagles receiver Torrey Smith (82) catches a touchdown pass in front of Vikings defenders Trae Waynes (26) and Harrison Smith (22). *AP Photo*

Eagles defensive end Derek Barnett (96) strips the ball from Vikings quarterback Case Keenum (7) during the second quarter. *AP Photo*

champion Patriots in two weeks.

And maybe it's time for everyone to put aside Carson Wentz's injury. Nick Foles might be good enough to win the Eagles their first NFL title since 1960.

Foles was on fire Sunday night against the stingiest scoring defense in the NFL. Next up after their most-lopsided playoff victory: the Eagles' first Super Bowl appearance since 2005, against the team that beat them then.

Foles replaced the injured Wentz in Game 13 and finished off a rise from last place last season to first in the NFC East. There were plenty of doubters entering the playoffs, but the former starter in Philadelphia (15-3) under another regime has been brilliant.

"I just think you've got to keep going at it," Foles said. "And we all believe in each other. I'm blessed to have amazing teammates, amazing coaches. Everyone here that's a part

of the Philadelphia Eagles organization is first class."

Foles' best work might have come against Minnesota (14-4) and its vaunted defense that was torn apart in every manner. Foles threw for 352 yards and three touchdowns, showing poise, escapability and moxie in going 26 for 33.

"I'm so happy for Nick and the offense," said Eagles coach Doug Pederson, "and for Nick, everything he's been through and battled, he stayed the course and we all believed in him."

Foles was helped greatly by the Eagles' domination on defense and a spectacular weaving 50-yard interception return TD by Patrick Robinson. Philadelphia ruined the Vikings' hopes of being the first team to play in a Super Bowl in its own stadium.

"I'm so proud of our players," team owner

WORLD CHAMPIONS

103

Eagles defensive tackle Destiny Vaeao (97) brings down Vikings running back Jerick McKinnon (21) during the second half. *AP Photo*

Vikings quarterback Case Keenum (7) attempts a pass as he falls after barely avoiding the Eagles rush. *AP Photo*

Jeffrey Lurie said. "The resilience this group of men has is unequaled."

Minnesota made it look easy at the outset, driving 75 yards on nine plays, each of which gained yardage. The payoff was a 25-yard throw from Case Keenum to Kyle Rudolph well behind linebacker Najee Goode as Philadelphia's defense looked confused on the play.

That didn't happen again for Philly.

Defensive end Chris Long had a huge hand in Robinson's 50-yard interception return. Long burst in from the left side and got his arm on Keenum to disrupt the throw for Adam Thielen. The ball went directly to Robinson, who sped down the left side, then made a sharp cut to the right and got a superb block from Ronald Darby to reach the end zone.

Inspired, Philly's D forced a three-and-out, the Foles led the Eagles on a 12-play, 75-yard masterpiece of a drive. LeGarrette

Blount showed all his power and escapability on an 11-yard surge up the middle for a 14-7 lead.

Turnovers, something Minnesota rarely committed with an NFC-low 14 during the season, hurt again and not only ended a solid drive, but set up more Philly points. On third down from the Eagles 15, Keenum was blindsided by rookie Derek Barnett, and the ball bounced directly to Long.

It was only the second strip-sack the Vikings have been victimized by all season.

A blown coverage - another rarity for Minnesota - on third-and-10 allowed Alshon Jeffery to get wide open for a 53-yard TD, and Philadelphia tacked on Jake Elliott's 38-yard field goal to make it 24-3 at halftime.

"Credit to Philadelphia, they got after us pretty good tonight and we didn't do enough good things," Vikings coach Mike Zimmer said.

Jeffery caught TD passes of 53 and 5 yards

Beau Allen (94) and Chris Long (56) don their dog masks to remind everyone the Eagles were the underdogs in the NFC Championship game. *AP Photo*

BOX SCORE

	1	2	3	4	T
Minnesota	7	0	0	0	7
Philadelphia	7	17	7	7	38

GAME LEADERS

PASSING YARDS

MIN	C. Keenum	28-48, 271 YDS, 1 TD, 2 INT
PHI	N. Foles	26-33, 352 YDS, 3 TD

RUSHING YARDS

MIN	J. McKinnon	10 CAR, 40 YDS
PHI	J. Ajayi	18 CAR, 73 YDS

RECEIVING YARDS

MIN	J. McKinnon	11 REC, 86 YDS
PHI	Z. Ertz	8 REC, 93 YDS

and had five receptions for 85 yards. Ertz was free seemingly all night and finished with eight catches for 93 yards. Torrey Smith had a 41-yard TD catch against double coverage in the third period.

"We've got an amazing coaching staff especially offensively. Flip (quarterbacks coach John DeFilippo) is an amazing coach. Frank Reich. All these guys are established offensive coordinators and they go into the lab and they draw up stuff I never even thought possible, and then we come here on Tuesday, Wednesday, Thursday, Friday with the game plan and I'm like, 'Hey, we've got a good shot,'" Ertz said.

"They do an amazing job of just putting us in position to be successful and that's all you can ask for as a player." ∎

QUARTERBACK
CARSON WENTZ

Wentz Still Looks to Inspire

In a little over a month, Carson Wentz has gone from a likely MVP quarterback to an inspirational cheerleader for his Eagles teammates.

And as much as Wentz is enjoying the Eagles' ride to the Super Bowl, he has to be hurting inside that he can't be taking part in it. Wentz tore his ACL on Dec. 10 in a game against the Los Angeles Rams, ending his season.

Wentz can be seen on the sideline during the games, walking with a cane, cheering on his teammates while Nick Foles has gone 4-1 in his place, including playoff wins over the Atlanta Falcons and Minnesota Vikings.

"To me, one of the greatest things about a person that you can say is when you see him celebrating somebody else's success," Eagles offensive coordinator Frank Reich said. "Even when you know it's at the same position. I don't care, human nature tells you that's hard to do, and it's been fun to see those two do that.

"It's fun to see Carson have the maturity to truly celebrate Nick's success and understanding how he's helping this team, and also with the frustration knowing that he wants to be in there."

Wentz has not commented publicly since the injury. But his teammates have said that Wentz is at the team's practice facility every day, at least in the mornings, doing his rehab, participating in meetings and talking to his teammates.

Foles, for one, has said that Wentz has been very helpful in preparing him to take over. So when the Eagles' 38-7 win over the Minnesota Vikings in the NFC Championship game was complete, Foles and Wentz were seen hugging on the sideline.

When asked what was said during that embrace, Foles responded: "Carson and I have worked together this entire year and he's a huge reason why we're in this position. It's been awesome just being around him. He's handled this thing amazingly and he continues to be such a great leader in our locker room.

Carson Wentz looks on as Nick Foles warms up before the divisional playoff game against Atlanta. *AP Photo*

Eagles quarterback Nick Foles (right) hugs injured quarterback Carson Wentz (left) after the NFC Conference Championship game. *AP Photo*

"When we go through game film and we go through everything, he's an extremely intelligent player so I listen to everything that he says. In that moment, you just embrace. It's been a crazy year and we work together every single day for long hours. You don't really need to say anything. A hug goes a long way."

Before his injury, Wentz was already having a historic season for an Eagles quarterback. He played in the Eagles' first 13 games, and led the team to an 11-2 record. He threw for 3,296 yards and was on pace to become the first quarterback in team history to surpass 4,000 yards passing in a season.

Wentz had thrown for 33 touchdowns, breaking a team record set by Sonny Jurgensen in 1961. In fact, Wentz's last pass of the season, a 2-yard TD pass to Alshon Jeffery late in the third quarter against the Rams, was the record breaker.

Wentz threw just seven interceptions in those 13 games, and had a quarterback rating of 101.9, which was fourth best in the NFL at the time.

Foles replaced Wentz after that. He threw four touchdown passes in his first start, against the Giants on Dec. 17. But Foles struggled in the next two regular-season games leading up to the playoffs.

But Foles has played much better once the postseason began, most notably in the win over the Vikings. Foles completed 26 of 33 passes, including all 11 attempts in the second half, for 352 yards with 3 TDs and no interceptions against the Vikings. Foles had a QB rating of 141.1.

Wentz certainly had a role in that. Reich said he told Wentz that in the fourth quarter against the Vikings when the game was already well in hand.

"He's been outstanding," Reich said. "Just kind of reminding him of, obviously, the incredibly important role that he's played in everything... It's absolutely human to wish that you were in there. But the whole key, it's a very fine line. And that fine line to me is that you can still not just be happy for the team winning, but to be happy for Nick who is at your position, who could potentially be stealing another person's thunder.

"But that's the pretty cool thing. Of all the great things that he's done this year, [this] even more exemplifies the kind of leader that he is." ∎

PATRIOTS AND EAGLES
get settled in Minnesota as Super Bowl LII approaches

The New England Patriots and Philadelphia Eagles began settling in Monday for a hectic and chilly week of Super Bowl preparations.

The Patriots, seeking their sixth Super Bowl title in eight appearances in the big game with Tom Brady as their quarterback and Bill Belichick as their coach, were greeted by frigid temperatures and snow on the ground when they arrived in the Minneapolis area Monday. The Eagles, in pursuit of their first Super Bowl triumph, landed Sunday.

Both teams are scheduled to participate in media night activities later Monday, when the excesses of the Super Bowl buildup usually are on the most vivid display. From there, the Patriots and Eagles will make themselves at home in hotels near the massive Mall of America, where the media center for the week has been set up in reclaimed retail space alongside stores and restaurants.

The NFL certainly could use a compelling Super Bowl to make fans forget about major injuries during the regular season to high-profile NFL stars such as Carson Wentz, Aaron Rodgers, Deshaun Watson, Odell Beckham Jr., J.J. Watt and Richard Sherman.

The presence of the Patriots certainly helps. They are the team most everyone either loves or loves to hate, and they will attempt to add more on-field glory to their complicated legacy that weaves together championships and scandals. They seek to win a third Super Bowl title in a four-year span for the second time during the era of Brady and Belichick.

The Eagles arrive in their now-familiar underdog role even after being the No. 1 seed in the NFC playoffs and overwhelming the Minnesota Vikings in the NFC title game in Philadelphia to prevent a Super Bowl first of having the local team playing the game on its home field. Quarterback Nick Foles, thrust into the starting role in December, will attempt to recreate the magical passing touch he had against the Vikings.

But this time, the opponent is the Patriots. Belichick and defensive coordinator Matt Patricia will have had nearly two weeks to get their defense ready. For Foles and the Eagles, the task is daunting.

"I focus on the team," Foles said Monday night. "That's all I care about, just living in the moment, especially what I've gone through the last couple years and what I've seen and my perspective. … I'm grateful for the moment. The future can take care of itself, because right now we've got a lot going on." ∎

Injured Eagles quarterback Carson Wentz, front, arrives in Minneapolis with his teammates for Super Bowl 52. *AP Photo*

TALE OF THE TAPE

2017 REGULAR SEASON	NEW ENGLAND	PHILADELPHIA
Record	13-3	13-3
Divisional Standings	1st	1st
Total Yards Gained	6,307	5,852
Total Offense (Rank)	394.2 (1)	365.8 (7)
Rush Offense	118.1 (10)	132.2 (3)
Pass Offense	276.1 (2)	233.6 (13)
Points Per Game	28.6 (2)	28.6 (3)
Touchdowns Scored	49	53
Third Down Conversion Pct.	40.6	41.7
Total Yards Allowed	5,856	4,904
Total Defense (Rank)	366.0 (29)	306.5 (4)
Rush Defense	114.8 (20)	79.2 (1)
Pass Defense	251.3 (30)	227.3 (17)
Points Allowed/ Game	18.5 (5)	18.4 (4)

2017 REGULAR SEASON	NEW ENGLAND	PHILADELPHIA
Touchdowns Allowed	33	34
Third Down Defense (Pct.)	39.4	32.2
Field Goals Made/ Attempted	37/40	29/34
Possession Avg.	30:37	32:41
Sacks Allowed/Yards Lost	35/201	36/230
Sacks Made/Yards	42/299	38/246
Passing TD/INT. (Off.)	32/8	38/9
Passing TD/INT. (DEF)	24/12	24/19
Penalties Against/ Yards	95/835	116/962
Punts/Avg.	58/43.4	68/44.6
Turnover Differential	+6 (11)	+11 (4)

The Philadelphia Eagles are introduced on stage. *AP Photo*

Eagles running back Jay Ajayi is interviewed during Super Bowl LII Opening Night. *AP Photo*

Fletcher Cox wears his green wrestling mask as he takes part in media interviews. *AP Photo*

The elusive –and costly – Super Bowl 52 tickets, *AP Photo*

Fans start to filter into the U.S. Bank Stadium in Minneapolis, Minnesota before the beginning of Super Bowl LII between the Eagles and Patriots. *AP Photo*

Eagles wide receiver Alshon Jeffery (17) makes a 34-yard touchdown reception over Patriots cornerback Eric Rowe (25) during the first half. *AP Photo*

EAGLES
PATRIOTS

41
33

SUPER
BOWL
LII

Feb. 4 vs. New England   U.S. Bank Stadium   Minneapolis, Minnesota

Tight end Zach Ertz celebrates on stage following the Eagles victory over the Patriots in Super Bowl LII. *AP Photo*

World Champions!

As their delirious fans sang their theme song and their owner lifted the Lombardi Trophy, the Philadelphia Eagles' finally could breathe freely.

Quarterback Nick Foles guided the drive of a lifetime, Zach Ertz made a bobbling touchdown catch that had to survive replay review, and an exhausted defense came up with not one but two stands in the final moments Sunday for a 41-33 victory over Tom Brady and the favored New England Patriots.

Eagles running back LeGarrette Blount (29), left, drags Patriots strong safety Duron Harmon into the end zone on his 21-yard touchdown run. *AP Photo*

For the first time since 1960, the Eagles are NFL champions. That would be fifty-eight years; 20,859 days; more than two generations. For a fan base whose loyalty has not wavered amid endless heartbreak, the drought is mercifully over. And the party is on.

"Fly Eagles Fly," indeed.

"We've played this game since we were little kids, we dreamed about this moment," game MVP Foles said. "There's plenty of kids watching this game right now dreaming about this moment and someday will be here."

In a record-setting Super Bowl shootout between backup QB Foles and five-time champ Brady, Foles led a pressure-packed 75-yard drive to the winning touchdown, an 11-yard pass to Ertz with 2:21 to go.

Then Brandon Graham came up with the defensive play-of-the-game when he strip-sacked Brady and Derek Barnett recovered, setting up rookie Jake Elliot's 46-yard field goal for an 8-point lead.

Brady got his team to midfield on the final drive, but his desperation pass fell to the ground in the end zone.

"For us, it was all about one stop we had to make. We went out and made that one stop," Graham said.

Eagles safety Malcolm Jenkins (27) delivers a big hit on Patriots receiver Brandin Cooks (14) during the first half. *AP Photo*

Eagles quarterback Nick Foles (9) catches a touchdown pass from teammate Trey Burton (86) on a key fourth down play late in the first half. *AP Photo*

The underdog Eagles (16-3), even injured starting quarterback Carson Wentz, came bolting off the sideline in ecstasy while Brady sat on the ground, disconsolate.

It was the first Super Bowl title for Philadelphia (16-3), which went 7-9 last season.

"If there's a word (it's) called everything," Eagles owner Jeffrey Lurie said. "That's what it means to Eagles fans everywhere. And for Eagles fans everywhere, this is for them."

Super Bowl MVP Foles orchestrated the victory with the kind of drive NFL MVP Brady,

a five-time champion, is known for. The drive covered 14 plays, including a fourth-down conversion.

"I felt calm. I mean, we have such a great group of guys, such a great coaching staff," Foles said. "We felt confident coming in, and we just went out there and played football."

The Eagles had to survive a video replay because the ball popped into the air as Ertz crossed the goal line.

"If they would have overturned that, I don't know what would have happened to the city of

▲ Rookie running back Corey Clements (30) makes a touchdown catch in the back of the end zone. *AP Photo*

▼ Eagles tight end Zach Ertz (86) dives into the end zone over Patriots free safety Devin McCourty (32) for a touchdown. *AP Photo*

▲Patriots tight end Rob Gronkowski (87) beats Eagles cornerback Ronald Darby (41) for a touchdown reception. *AP Photo*

▼Eagles wide receiver Nelson Agholor (13) fights off Patriots cornerback Johnson Bademosi (29) to make the catch. *AP Photo*

Eagles defensive end Brandon Graham makes the defensive play of the game by stripping Patriots quarterback Tom Brady (12). The Eagles recovered the fumble. *AP Photo*

Philadelphia," Ertz said. "But I'm so glad they didn't overturn it."

The touchdown stood — and so did thousands of green-clad Eagles fans who weren't going to mind the frigid conditions outside US Bank Stadium once they headed out to celebrate.

The Patriots (15-4) seemed ready to take their sixth championship with Brady and coach Bill Belichick in eight Super Bowls. Brady threw for a game-record 505 yards and three TDs, hitting Rob Gronkowski for 4 yards before Stephen Gostkowski's extra point gave New England its first lead, 33-32.

Then Foles made Philadelphia fans forget about Eagles injured starting quarterback CarsonWentz — at least for now — with the gutsiest drive of his life.

"We couldn't make a play to give the ball back to the offense," Patriots cornerback Stephon Gilmore said.

Foles has been something of a journeyman in his six pro seasons, but he has been spectacular in four career playoff games. He finished 28 of 43 for 373 yards and three TDs.

The combined 1,151 yards were the most in any modern NFL game, and Brady's 505 were the most in any playoff contest. The 40-year-old master finished 28 of 48 and picked apart the Eagles until the final two series.

It was such a wild game that Foles caught a touchdown pass, and Brady would have if he had been able to hang on to the Danny Amendola throw that went off his fingertips.

Brady and the Patriots looked ready for another comeback by opening the second half

Eagles defenders make sure the Patriots final Hail Mary isn't answered. *AP Photo*

BOX SCORE

	1	2	3	4	T
Philadelphia	9	13	7	12	41
New England	3	9	14	7	33

GAME LEADERS

PASSING YARDS
PHI	N. Foles	28-43, 373 YDS, 3 TD, 1 INT
NE	T. Brady	28-48, 505 YDS, 3 TD

RUSHING YARDS
PHI	L. Blount	14 CAR, 90 YDS, 1 TD
NE	J. White	7 CAR, 45 YDS, 1 TD

RECEIVING YARDS
PHI	C. Clement	4 REC, 100 YDS, 1 TD
NE	D. Amendola	8 REC, 152 YDS

with a 75-yard touchdown drive. Gronkowski was unstoppable, grabbing four passes for 69 yards, including the 5-yard score.

Philly didn't flinch, answering with a precise 75-yard march and three more third-down conversions - the Eagles were 10 for 16 on third down for the game. Foles perfect pass to Corey Clement over double coverage –the rookie's reception was upheld by review—put the Eagles back on top by 10.

Brady came right back and, getting steadfast protection, connected with Chris Hogan from the 26 for another touchdown.

When all the Eagles could manage was Elliott's 42-yarder for a 32-26 lead, it seemed inevitable the Patriots would go in front, then become the first repeat Super Bowl winner since they did it in the 2004 and '05 games.

Foles, Ertz, and — at last — a revitalized defense said otherwise. ∎

LeGarrette Blount and teammates pose with the Lombardi Trophy. *AP Photo*

Nate Gerry celebrates. *AP Photo*

General manager Howie Roseman, left, holds up the Vince Lombardi Trophy as he celebrates with head coach Doug Pederson, center, and owner Jeffrey Lurie, *AP Photo*

Nick Foles celebrates with his daughter Lily. *AP Photo*

EAGLES ROSTER 2017-2018

#	NAME	POS.	HT.	WT.	AGE	EXP.	COLLEGE
13	Agholor, Nelson	WR	6-0	198	24	3	USC
36	Ajayi, Jay	RB	6-0	223	24	3	Boise State
94	Allen, Beau	DT	6-3	327	26	4	Wisconsin
38	Barner, Kenjon	RB	5-9	195	28	4	Oregon
96	Barnett, Derek	DE	6-3	259	21	R	Tennessee
66	Beatty, Will	T	6-6	319	32	9	Connecticut
29	Blount, LeGarrette	RB	6-0	250	31	8	Oregon
53	Bradham, Nigel	LB	6-2	241	28	6	Florida State
50	Braman, Bryan	DE	6-5	241	30	7	West Texas A&M
79	Brooks, Brandon	G	6-5	335	28	6	Miami (Ohio)
88	Burton, Trey	TE	6-3	235	26	4	Florida
87	Celek, Brent	TE	6-4	255	33	11	Cincinnati
30	Clement, Corey	RB	5-10	220	23	R	Wisconsin
91	Cox, Fletcher	DT	6-4	310	27	6	Mississippi State
75	Curry, Vinny	DE	6-3	279	29	6	Marshall
41	Darby, Ronald	CB	5-11	193	24	3	Florida State
32	Douglas, Rasul	CB	6-2	209	22	R	West Virginia
57	Ellerbe, Dannell	LB	6-1	245	32	9	Georgia
4	Elliott, Jake	K	5-9	170	23	R	Memphis
86	Ertz, Zach	TE	6-5	250	27	5	Stanford
9	Foles, Nick	QB	6-6	243	29	6	Arizona
47	Gerry, Nathan	LB	6-2	218	22	R	Nebraska
18	Gibson, Shelton	WR	5-11	191	22	R	West Virginia
52	Goode, Najee	LB	6-0	244	28	6	West Virginia
55	Graham, Brandon	DE	6-2	265	29	8	Michigan
24	Graham, Corey	S	6-0	196	32	10	New Hampshire
54	Grugier-Hill, Kamu	LB	6-2	220	23	2	Eastern Illinois
10	Hollins, Mack	WR	6-4	221	24	R	North Carolina
17	Jeffery, Alshon	WR	6-3	218	27	6	South Carolina
27	Jenkins, Malcolm	S	6-0	204	30	9	Ohio State
93	Jernigan, Tim	DT	6-2	295	25	4	Florida State
65	Johnson, Lane	T	6-6	317	27	5	Oklahoma
14	Johnson, Marcus	WR	6-1	204	23	1	Texas
8	Jones, Donnie	P	6-2	221	37	14	LSU
22	Jones, Sidney	CB	6-0	181	21	R	Washington
62	Kelce, Jason	C	6-3	295	30	7	Cincinnati
95	Kendricks, Mychal	LB	6-0	240	27	6	California
56	Long, Chris	DE	6-3	270	32	10	Virginia
45	Lovato, Rick	LS	6-2	249	25	1	Old Dominion
23	McLeod, Rodney	S	5-10	195	27	6	Virginia
51	Means, Steven	DE	6-3	263	27	3	Buffalo
31	Mills, Jalen	CB	6-0	191	23	2	LSU
98	Qualls, Elijah	DT	6-1	321	22	R	Washington
21	Robinson, Patrick	CB	5-11	191	30	8	Florida State
73	Seumalo, Isaac	G	6-4	303	24	2	Oregon State
28	Smallwood, Wendell	RB	5-10	208	24	2	West Virginia
82	Smith, Torrey	WR	6-0	205	29	7	Maryland
7	Sudfeld, Nate	QB	6-6	227	24	2	Indiana
97	Vaeao, Destiny	DT	6-4	299	24	2	Washington State
72	Vaitai, Halapoulivaati	T	6-6	320	24	2	TCU
67	Warmack, Chance	G	6-2	323	26	5	Alabama
26	Watkins, Jaylen	S	5-11	194	26	3	Florida
61	Wisniewski, Stefen	G/C	6-3	305	28	7	Penn State

Reserve/Injured

#	NAME	POS.	HT.	WT.	AGE	EXP.	COLLEGE
	Goforth, Randall	CB	5-10	190	24	R	UCLA
58	Hicks, Jordan	LB	6-1	236	25	3	Texas
42	Maragos, Chris	S	5-10	200	31	8	Wisconsin
71	Peters, Jason	T	6-4	328	36	14	Arkansas
34	Pumphrey, Donnel	RB	5-9	176	23	R	San Diego State
	Shittu, Aziz	DT	6-2	288	23	1	Stanford
43	Sproles, Darren	RB	5-6	190	34	13	Kansas State
6	Sturgis, Caleb	K	5-9	192	28	5	Florida
59	Walker, Joe	LB	6-2	236	25	2	Oregon
11	Wentz, Carson	QB	6-5	237	25	2	North Dakota State
	Williams, Dom	WR	6-2	200	25	1	Washington State